Steam Routes around
GLOUCESTER

and

LYDNEY • SHARPNESS • STROUD • SAPPERTON

An historic location, Tramway Junction was a favourite spot to observe and photograph the seemingly constant procession of trains coming and going – not to mention lots of shunting movements, adding to frustrating delays for motorists and others trying to proceed along Horton Road. Unusually, all signals appear to be 'on' possibly due to a problem at the road crossing requiring the use of a flagman as Collett 2-8-0 3866 steams underneath the gantry on an up freight past the GW loco shed. 4F 0-6-0 43887 waits to resume a shunting movement on the Midland side.

B W L Brooksbank, Initial Photographics

STEPHEN MOURTON

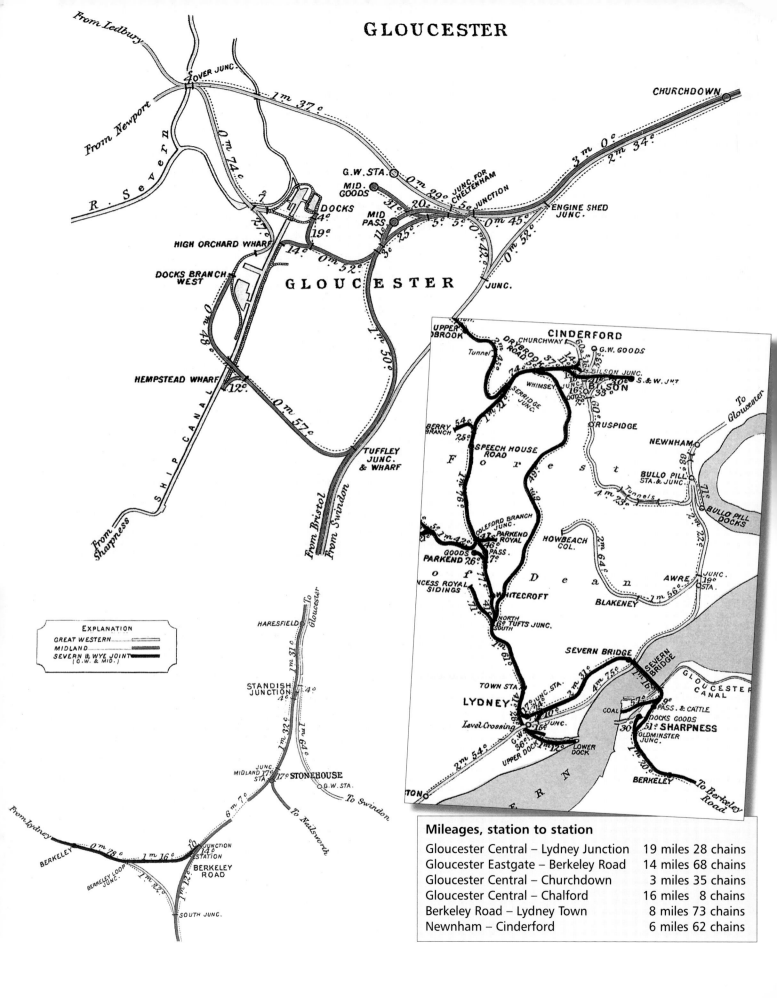

GLOUCESTER

Mileages, station to station

Gloucester Central – Lydney Junction	19 miles 28 chains
Gloucester Eastgate – Berkeley Road	14 miles 68 chains
Gloucester Central – Churchdown	3 miles 35 chains
Gloucester Central – Chalford	16 miles 8 chains
Berkeley Road – Lydney Town	8 miles 73 chains
Newnham – Cinderford	6 miles 62 chains

EXPLANATION
GREAT WESTERN
MIDLAND
SEVERN & WYE JOINT
(G.W. & MID.)

CONTENTS

Front cover: Gleaming Gloucester Horton Road based 7035 *Ogmore Castle* heads the 11.45am Cheltenham Spa to London Paddington express at Brimscombe in July 1962.   *Alan Jarvis*

Back cover, top: Lines in the Forest of Dean fed lots of traffic into Gloucester over the years and an ex-GWR 0-6-0PT provides power for this working on the Cinderford branch at the relatively substantial Ruspidge Halt in September 1965.

Back cover, bottom: The Midland presence at Gloucester is represented by the last of Barnwood's Compound 4-4-0s, 41123, which, coupled to a 'Jubilee' 4-6-0, waits to go to shed having brought the Newcastle-Cardiff train into Central station in the late 1950s.
John Tarrant, Kidderminster Railway Museum

Facing page: Pre-grouping *Railway Clearing House* maps of the area.

© 2006 Stephen Mourton

Published by Runpast Publishing, 10 Kingscote Grove, Cheltenham, Gloucestershire GL51 6JX

Typesetting and reproduction by Viners Wood Associates
Printed in England by The Amadeus Press Ltd., Cleckheaton

ISBN 1 870754 67 0

INTRODUCTION

It is now forty years since the railway at Gloucester saw steam locomotives on a daily basis, but the memory lingers, assisted by the occasional appearance nowadays of preserved engines on special workings.

The intention of this book is to preserve those images of bygone times when Gloucester and the surrounding area witnessed a great number of steam locos on many types of train every day. It also depicts some of the infrastructure of the steam era, such as long-gone stations and yards. Lines covered are those in and around the city of Gloucester, views along the main lines to Berkeley Road; Churchdown; Lydney; Sapperton and a brief look at some of the branches such as Bullo Pill to Cinderford; Lydney to Berkeley Road; Stonehouse to Stroud and Nailsworth.

With two loco sheds, two stations, the docks and numerous yards, there was rarely a dull moment on the Gloucester railway scene. The crossing gates at Barton Street and Horton Road were kept very busy as trains made their way in and out, not to mention seemingly constant shunting movements obstructing road traffic.

A goodly, and changing, variety of Great Western, Midland and British Railways Standard locomotives could be observed – just about every class apart from the biggest, while extra interest was generated by the appearance of a few ex-LNER types. Summer Saturdays were very busy, with some trains taking the Gloucester loop line, thus bypassing Eastgate station. Immaculate locos fresh from Swindon Works were seen on running-in turns.

Freight traffic was always brisk, particularly between the heavy industries of the Midlands and South Wales, coal and steel going in both directions. Although the opening of the Severn Tunnel in the 1880s meant Gloucester was no longer on the main line between London and South Wales, numerous freights between those places still slogged their way up Sapperton bank.

The photographs depict changes over the decades and include scenes from the pre-grouping era; from the post-grouping years – and from the BR period up to the cessation of everyday steam activity in the 1960s.

A lot of the railway infrastructure in Gloucester and Gloucestershire as seen in this book has now disappeared; not just the locomotives, but stations, junctions, signal boxes, engine sheds, yards. And the lifetime job on the railway, pursued by generations of the same family, has also gone as well, along with the social aspects of the railway community, which so often seemed to go hand-in-hand with the pride in a task well done.

Right: A spruce looking 6832 *Brockton Grange* powers its train of vans from South Wales out of the up loop at Over in 1962. The line to Docks Branch Sidings is on the left, while the signals behind the train indicate the Ledbury branch, shorn of its passenger service by this date and cut back to Dymock. Thomas Telford's fine road bridge, opened in 1831, dominates on the right. The more modest railway bridge was realigned in the 1950s, but still posed a big engineering challenge. *N E Preedy*

Below: The two stations at Gloucester had contrasting exteriors, reflecting the architectural styles of the Midland Railway (right) and the Great Western Railway (left). Both were simply called 'Gloucester' before nationalisation. Eastgate station has a modern addition on its right-hand side and both were required to accomodate motor vehicles on their forecourts in these views taken in May 1973. While Eastgate was later totally swept away, Central was rebuilt, though parts of the old station platforms are recognisable from steam days and remain in use today. *RCTS*

HISTORICAL SURVEY

Main lines and branches

The railway layout at Gloucester has proved problematical from the earliest days to the present time. Today, there is a lobby for a new Parkway type station at Elmbridge Court, Gloucester because a lot of cross-country services use the loop line to avoid reversal at the current Gloucester station. This deprives the citizenry of important cross-country services, unless they travel to Cheltenham and change there, increasing journey times and, of course, inconvenience. In the earliest days of railways in the city, even greater problems arose as it was a meeting place for standard and broad gauges from 1844, which caused chaos for passengers and goods, focussing national attention on the problem, including a skit in the satirical magazine '*Punch*' and its depiction in well-known and much reproduced drawings in '*The Illustrated London News*'. This led to a Parliamentary investigation, the 'Gauge Commission', and the eventual death knell for Brunel's broad gauge system. Changing trains at Gloucester was even necessary for Queen Victoria when she travelled through the city a couple of times – it is rumoured to have put her off a formal visit for the entirety of her long reign!

To add to the operating difficulties in those early days, the standard and broad gauge stations in the centre of Gloucester – situated close to the current Gloucester station – were originally termini, so trains had to reverse. The Great Western Railway station became a through one with the opening of the line to Grange Court and Chepstow in 1851. Trains between Birmingham and Bristol were, however, still faced with a reversal at the Midland Railway (MR) station until it built a new through station in 1896, albeit on a sharp curve. The GWR applied to build a new station at Chequers Road in the first decade of the twentieth century so that trains on its new Birmingham to Bristol service had a Gloucester stop, but the plan was turned down by Gloucester Corporation.

But Gloucester did develop as a major railway centre, thanks in part to an older form of transport – the waterways. Before the coming of the railway to Gloucester, its inland docks were important for its commercial well-being. For example, coal from the Forest of Dean could be brought in for use in the city or onward transportation by road or on the 3'6" tram road which linked the city with Cheltenham; it also enabled stone quarried at the latter place to be transported to the docks for movement by the Gloucester and Berkeley Canal to wherever it was needed. Nevertheless a railway was required to shift goods swiftly and economically to and from the rapidly expanding industries of Birmingham and the Midlands and this was the Birmingham & Gloucester, opened in November 1840, on the standard gauge. The section between

Above: The historic Gloucester 'T' Station building outwardly at least looks in good order in this April 1949 portrait, even though it had closed to passengers nearly a century earlier, in 1851. Regrettably the building was demolished in the BR era, so Gloucester lost this reminder of its early railway heritage. *S V Blencowe collection*

Cheltenham and Gloucester was the first new line of railway to be inspected prior to opening by the Board of Trade, on 21 October 1840, under recently introduced Parliamentary legislation. It was July 1844 when a broad gauge line, the Bristol & Gloucester, opened from Bristol to Standish Junction where it joined the Great Western Railway broad gauge from Swindon (originally the Cheltenham & Great Western Union) – though the Bristol & Gloucester had to construct the short Millstream Junction to Tramway Junction curve at Gloucester to access its platform adjacent to the Birmingham & Gloucester's. In fact the curve proved too sharp for the first train to the opening ceremony on 6 July – it derailed and no less a personage than Isambard Kingdom Brunel had to spend time supervising the repairs. However there were now opportunities for shifting freight and passengers between Bristol and Birmingham by rail. The GWR started running trains through from London and Swindon to Gloucester over the ex-Cheltenham & Great Western Union broad gauge in May 1845. This line over the Cotswolds had not been the easiest to construct, even with I K Brunel as Engineer, being steeply graded and having nine timber built viaducts, plus a long tunnel at Sapperton. It was laid on longitudinal sleepers, whereas Midland lines in the area had the more familiar transverse type.

It should be noted that for a while there were three gauges at Tramway Junction – the 3'6" of the Cheltenham & Gloucester tram road; the standard gauge of the Birmingham & Gloucester Railway; and the broad gauge of the Bristol & Gloucester Railway and Great Western Railway!

Much to the chagrin of the GWR, the Midland Railway managed to lease and then absorb both the Birmingham & Gloucester and Bristol & Gloucester companies, full amalgamation taking place on 3 August 1846. It was 1847 when the GWR started running its broad gauge trains to a new terminus station in Cheltenham – over the first dual gauge joint line in the country. But the GWR did not want its London Paddington to Cheltenham trains having to reverse at Gloucester, hence the construction east of the city of a bypass loop line and the so-called 'T' station thereon, where carriages were detached, put on a turntable and hauled into the city station, a state of affairs which lasted until 1851. In 1848 the Midland opened its branch from Tramway Junction, Gloucester to High Orchard yard in the docks, facilitating the transfer of goods which had, since mid-1844, utilised part of the Cheltenham & Gloucester tram road straddled by standard gauge edge rails and worked by horses. The Docks Branch Sidings line from Over to Llanthony came into operation in 1854, built by the GWR for the Gloucester & Dean Forest Railway, and was initially broad gauge. The Gloucester & Dean Forest Railway (later South Wales Railway) also had the broad gauge line from Gloucester to Grange Court. The latter place became the junction between the important South Wales line, opened in July 1852 for through trains, following completion of Brunel's suspension bridge over the River Wye at Chepstow, and the branch to Hereford

which was finally completed in June 1855.

In May 1854 the Midland Railway opened the Stonehouse Junction Railway, a standard gauge line from Gloucester to Tuffley and Standish Junction via Painswick Road; the route from Standish Junction to Bristol had already been converted to dual gauge, enabling standard gauge working throughout from Birmingham. This effected a great time saving at Gloucester for both passengers and goods, though the five level crossings between Tuffley and Gloucester station did nothing to endear this line to road users.

With the expansion of railways in the UK and around the world, the need for rolling stock saw the birth of an important undertaking in the city in 1860. Backed by local industrialists, this became the Gloucester Railway Carriage and Wagon Company, which manufactured rolling stock for over a hundred years, used on many railways at home and abroad. Its first Chairman, Richard Potter, who lived at Standish House, was for a time also Chairman of the Great Western Railway. The works was connected to the Midland Railway in Gloucester Docks and its products could be seen being towed to various ports for export to railways in far-off countries.

Below: The main line between Gloucester and Cheltenham has had two tracks for most of its existence, but was a bottleneck for the first hundred years. It was increased to four tracks in 1942 to better cope with heavy wartime traffic, but post-war cutbacks reduced it to two tracks again in 1966/67. 0-6-2T 6696 hauls a Paddington-Cheltenham train away from Churchdown in 1961. This class of loco was perhaps most associated with South Wales, but Gloucester Horton Road shed usually had one or two allocated for various duties, including the daily pick-up freight to Severn Tunnel Junction. *T E Williams*

Above: The Midland Railway had a network of lines in Gloucester Docks. In this scene dated 4 June 1962, Deeley 0-4-0T 41535 propels a load of timber along the High Orchard branch adjacent to Weston Road. This had probably come by train from Sharpness; another engine would bring it in off the main line before 41535 attached to the rear – hence the brake van next to the loco – and shunted the wagons into the dock sidings.

Bill Potter, Kidderminster Railway Museum

Below: Coaley Junction looks pleasantly tranquil and rural in this picture dated 1923 looking along the Midland main line towards Bristol from Gloucester. Although owned by the Midland Railway, the GWR had running powers over the section from Standish Junction to Yate, which occasionally caused some friction between the two railways. Note the tall posts hoisting the signals above the bridge in the background, to aid sighting by train drivers. Coaley was the junction for the two and a half mile branch to Cam and Dursley, with trains using a separate platform at the station. The main building seen here was erected for the Dursley & Midland Junction Railway which constructed the branch and opened it in 1856. The branch passenger ceased in September 1962, but freight for Listers of Dursley continued until July 1970. Today there is a modern station nearby on the main line, Cam and Dursley, opened in May 1994.

Stations UK

On the line to Bristol, the Midland worked the leased Stonehouse and Nailsworth Railway branch, which commenced operation in February 1867, being vested in the MR in 1878. A line from Dudbridge, on the Nailsworth branch, was constructed to Stroud, with goods trains allowed from November 1885 and passenger services from July 1886.

Further along the Bristol line, a short branch diverged from Dursley (later Coaley) Junction to Dursley. It was opened in 1856, but the MR worked it from May 1861. Conversion of the GWR's lines from broad to standard gauge started in the area in August 1869 with the branch from Grange Court to Hereford, while Docks Branch Siding was also converted in 1869. The changeover was essentially completed in May 1872 as far as Gloucester was concerned when the South Wales, Cheltenham and Swindon lines were converted. Another event in 1872 was the GWR opening its new locomotive shed at Horton Road, replacing one dating from 1851; further improvements, including a new coal stage, were made much later, in 1921.

The Severn Bridge Railway between Lydney and Sharpness was ready for trains in October 1879 which enabled coal from the Forest of Dean to bypass Gloucester and be transported to Bristol using the Midland Railway's link from the main line at Berkeley Road, opened for goods in August 1875 and passenger in August 1876. An even bigger change was the opening of the Severn Tunnel in 1886, which led to a gradual rerouting of many passenger and goods trains away from the old South Wales main line through Gloucester, though some services between London and South Wales continued to use the route throughout the steam era.

The construction of the new Midland station at Gloucester in 1896 was partly on the site of the MR's locomotive roundhouse and necessitated the construction of a new one, situated at Barnwood from July 1894. The New Docks Branch from Tuffley to Hempsted, used for goods only, was brought into use in May 1900.

The Gloucester loop line, closed in 1851, was resurrected by the GWR in 1901 for goods trains, and from 1 July 1908 for its new passenger service from Birmingham to Bristol via Honeybourne and Cheltenham, but not stopping at Gloucester. Earlier in 1908, the GWR started running on the Berkeley Loop, so that it could run trains direct from Bristol to Lydney, without the need for reversal at Berkeley Road.

The Second World War saw a further significant change, with the widening from two to four tracks of the Gloucester to Cheltenham section between May and August 1942. This had long been a bottleneck for trains with just one up and one down track, causing delays on this busy route, which were no longer acceptable in the

Above: One of the branches off the South Wales main line between Gloucester and Lydney went from Bullo Pill to Cinderford and it had a passenger service until 1 November 1958; freight services lasted well into the 1960s, with the branch closing in 1967. This scene is at Bilson Junction with the signalman preparing to hand the single line token to the fireman of the 0-6-0PT on its way back from Cinderford. Apart from Cinderford, there were freights at this time going beyond Bilson to Northern United Colliery and bitumen manufacturers Berry Wiggins at Whimsey.

wartime situation. A number of substantial new Air Raid Precaution type signal boxes were included in the reconstruction, as were alterations to Churchdown station.

Nationalisation in 1948 did not bring any immediate significant changes. But April 1950 saw regional boundary alterations with the Western Region tightening its grip in the area and in 1951 the two Gloucester stations were renamed – the GWR station became 'Central' and the LMS became 'Eastgate'.

As the 1950s progressed, older engines disappeared and BR Standard types became familiar, including those built at Swindon, often seen on running-in turns. BR modernisation plans announced in the mid 1950s forecast the total elimination of steam by the 1970s. Diesel multiple units took over some turns, not just local ones, but also Birmingham-South Wales expresses. Barnwood locomotive depot was transferred from the London Midland Region shed code of 22B to the Western Region's 85E and had ex-GW 0-6-0PT allocated. New diesel hydraulic locos were seen occasionally in the late 1950s and diesel shunters were at work in local yards.

But while there were still lots of trains to be seen, a gradual decline set in with lines losing passenger services, such as those from Gloucester to Cinderford, which ceased on and from 3 November 1958, leading to some stations and halts closing.

Into the 1960s, there was a proposal for a large new marshalling yard at Brookthorpe, between Gloucester and Haresfield, but this never came to fruition. Meanwhile both contraction of the local railway system and modernisation proceeded at a rapidly increasing rate. The area suffered significant closures both pre- and post-Beeching, not just branches, but closure of yards and main line stations as well. There were improvements – alterations to the layout at Standish Junction in autumn 1964 enabled Cheltenham to London trains to use Eastgate station, doing away with reversal at Central, with a saving in time and motive power. The Western Region felt able to announce the complete cessation of steam at Gloucester from the beginning of 1966 – this did not quite happen as planned, but BR steam activity was significantly reduced and petered out later in 1966. Many signal boxes were replaced in May 1968 by a new area power box situated alongside Horton Road crossing. Increasing delays to the ever-busier road traffic at Barton Street and other crossings on the line between Eastgate

Above: The GWR was faced with a stiff ascent of the Cotswolds on the Cheltenham & Great Western Union line from Standish Junction to Swindon. Many trains needed assistance on the climb up Sapperton bank, but not 5017 *The Gloucestershire Regiment 28th,61st* with 1A56, the 11.45am Cheltenham to Paddington. This was a turn for a Gloucester engine which spent the morning on shed being polished and pampered by a gang of cleaners so as to look its best for this duty. If assistance was required, another loco coupled on the front of the train engine on passengers, but for freights came on as a banker, not coupled, behind the brake van. *George Heiron, The Transport Treasury*

and Tuffley led to the elimination of this section and closure of Eastgate station in December 1975, meaning all passenger trains calling at Gloucester once again had to reverse at Central. This inconvenience caused some cross-country express trains to avoid Gloucester by using the loop line, and, in the current era of privatised railway operators, delays and slowings down are to be avoided whenever possible, so Gloucester suffers a reduced service on important long-distance routes.

TRAIN SERVICES

Freight Traffic

While Gloucester was not one of the most important places in England in the early 1800s for manufactured goods or extractive industries such as coal, which were ideal for transport by rail, it was a staging point for such traffic between South Wales, the Forest of Dean and London and the Midlands.

Connection to the railway system enabled, for example, salt from the Droitwich area to be sent out via the docks – where the Midland Railway constructed special chutes for the purpose. Vital raw material like copper was brought in from abroad for onward transport by rail to Midlands factories.

The GWR service timetable for June 1862 showed the section from Grange Court to Gloucester was busy with

goods from the South Wales Railway and Hereford; coal from Aberdare, Lydney and Bullo; the Irish Goods from Waterford. There were also eight coal, coke and goods trains from Swindon to Gloucester. As the railway connections through Gloucester expanded, the city witnessed huge tonnages of coal from South Wales to London passing through, hauled for many years by nothing bigger than double-headed 0-6-0ST.

Manufacturing industry in Gloucester itself was boosted considerably by the formation in 1860 of the company which became known the world over as the Gloucester Railway Carriage & Wagon Co. (GRCW) and was a major employer in the city for a hundred years. Its rolling stock was used on British railways including the London underground, as well as being exported to the British Empire and many other countries – it used to have a considerable wagon leasing operation in the USA in its earlier years and exported much stock to Russia. As a small example of the company's output, the *'Railway Observer'* recorded two streamlined railcars for the Central Argentine Railway being shipped to South Wales via Lydney behind GWR 'Mogul' 6381 on 11 July 1937. This was also the year when GRCW received the biggest single order ever placed by London Transport, 401 cars for the District and Metropolitan lines, which, on completion, were all towed to London by rail. A company called Wagon Repairs also set up in Gloucester to get a share of the lucrative market in maintaining the many thousands of private owner wagons which ran on the railways. Apart from the GWR and Midland Railway lines, the dock authority also had its own tracks. There were many private sidings in the docks and elsewhere, including those of GRCW, England's Glory Matches, and a number of corn merchants who had distinctive warehouses, some of which still survive.

A number of marshalling yards were laid out by the GWR and MR close to their passenger stations to shunt and sort wagons coming and going in all directions – trains from the north might have traffic for Bristol, Bath, the West of England, Swindon and South Wales, which needed to be separated into new trains for the onward journey.

Coal was shifted in all directions, from the Midlands, Forest of Dean and South Wales. The GWR had the Old Yard between its station and Horton Road loco shed; its goods shed was situated here. The 'T' sidings were located within the triangle formed by the Swindon, Cheltenham and Loop lines. Over the years these expanded into the New Yard. The MR had a big yard at Barnwood, close to its 1894 engine roundhouse, with Upper Yard and Eastgate Yard, where its goods shed was situated, adjacent to its passenger station. The GWR had Docks Branch Sidings at Over to sort traffic to and from the docks, also a yard at Llanthony. The MR's High Orchard branch to the docks was supplemented in 1900 by a branch from Tuffley to Hempsted to serve the industry in the New Docks there and Gloucester Gasworks, the latter thus being rail connected for the first time. It had previously had coal delivered on the waterways. Further out, Quedgeley became important in the First World War with the opening of a rail-connected munitions factory. A large RAF maintenance unit was located here in 1939, providing much rail traffic as did the Dowmac concrete plant opened in 1963, which made railway sleepers amongst other products. Wagons had to be shifted between all these yards, so there were a goodly number of transfer freights running throughout the day and night, to timetables as strict as long-distance express trains.

Being an important farming centre, there was a good traffic in livestock – the original B&G terminus station had been located very close to the cattle market – and all types of locally produced agricultural produce, with the addition of items from further afield like broccoli and potatoes from Penzance, and flowers from the Scilly Isles. Ale and porter were of course also important traffic for the railways for many years, with the 'Burton Beer' train coming through on weekdays to a fast schedule. Racing pigeons were transported by rail well into the 1960s to be released at various points to fly back home,

while trains of horseboxes, often complete with grooms, could be seen into late steam days. Parcels and mail trains called several times a day, including the Fishguard Harbour to Paddington working. The Christmas period would see many extra trains laid on for the purpose. The railway companies had fleets of road vehicles based at Gloucester to shift goods to places and customers not rail connected. Some horse-drawn transport survived into early BR days.

Passenger Traffic

It was 4 November 1840 when regular passenger trains commenced operation between Gloucester and Cheltenham; the journey took 16 minutes. Services which had been running from Cheltenham to Bromsgrove since June were extended to Camp Hill, Birmingham from mid-December, and into Curzon Street station from 14 August 1841. A month later, it was possible to book from Gloucester to London via the B&G and the London & Birmingham Railway, while over the next couple of years, through carriages were introduced for the journey. From 8 July 1844 passenger trains ran between Gloucester and Bristol. Another significant connection occurred the following year, on 12 May, when trains operated on the Cheltenham & Great Western Union line from Swindon into Gloucester via Standish Junction. But all these trains, full of passengers and their luggage, served to emphasise the chaos caused by the break of gauge.

By Summer 1860 the Midland Railway weekday passenger timetable showed five trains between Gloucester and Bristol, the fastest taking one hour fifteen minutes. From Gloucester to Birmingham there were six trains, with the swiftest taking a few minutes under two hours. Connections at Gloucester enabled travellers to get from West Wales to Newcastle-upon-Tyne on the same day. For example, departure from Swansea at 4.45am got a passenger to York by 4pm and Newcastle at 7.45pm. First and Second class passengers were allowed to travel on all trains, but third-class ones were restricted to certain services only. The Midland also advertised three weekday services from Gloucester to London in conjunction with the Oxford, Worcester & Wolverhampton Railway – one involved changing at Norton Junction rather than Worcester itself. The best time for the whole journey was five hours five minutes.

The GWR's June 1862 service timetable had eight daily passenger workings from Swindon to Gloucester – the best journey time from London took three hours twenty minutes to Gloucester. In addition, there were trains over the broad gauge to the GWR's Cheltenham terminus. Grange Court to Gloucester saw eleven passenger and mail trains on weekdays, including those from Hereford. There were also Sunday trains – the subject of some controversy with the Church authorities in earlier years.

The opening of the Somerset & Dorset Railway in 1874 meant new traffic flows on the line from Gloucester to Bristol as far as Mangotsfield, the junction for the Midland Railway branch to Bath, where it met the S&D. From 1880 it became possible to travel from Bournemouth to Gloucester without changing trains; through carriage workings were a big feature of Midland services and a passenger could go right through to, for example, Dundee, from Gloucester in the same seat.

After the opening of the Severn Tunnel in 1886, a number of trains were gradually diverted away from the Swindon-Gloucester-Severn Tunnel Junction line, with the new direct route saving over twenty-five miles. But it took quite a few years – for some time the fastest train to Cardiff, which left Paddington at 5.45pm, was still routed via Gloucester. It ran non-stop from Gloucester to Newport, the average journey speed being just under 45 miles an hour. All other expresses and mail trains on the Gloucester-Newport line stopped at Chepstow, and sometimes Lydney.

A significant boost for local passengers came in October 1903 when the GWR introduced steam rail motors between Chalford and Stonehouse; the service was soon extended to Gloucester and in later years became the familiar auto-train formed of a loco and one or more trailers, sometimes with the engine sandwiched in the middle. A number of small halts were also provided along the Stroud Valley.

In 1906 the GWR commenced the running of a long-distance train from South Wales to Newcastle-upon-Tyne, known as the 'Ports-to-Ports Express' After coming up the old South Wales main line to Gloucester, it took the Cheltenham to Banbury route and onto the Great Central Railway northwards. This survived until the start of the War in September 1939. The GWR introduced its own Birmingham-Bristol service in the summer of 1908, though this was of little use to Gloucester passengers as these trains passed through non-stop on the loop line. However, the competition did make the Midland smarten up its own services, which was of benefit to Gloucester. In 1910, in conjunction with the London & North Western Railway, a new train ran from Manchester to Bournemouth via Birmingham

Above: Perhaps the most interesting long-distance service at the GWR station was the South Wales to Newcastle 'Ports-to-Ports' express, which commenced operation in 1906, running north via the Cheltenham to Banbury line before joining the Great Central route and traversing Leicester, Nottingham and Sheffield on the way to its destination. A picture taken in 1907 sees this train, hauled by 'Bulldog' 4-4-0 3708, leaving Gloucester with a set of Great Central Railway coaches. Note the elevated signal cabin in the background.

Coutanche collection

and Gloucester – from 1927 it was named 'The Pines Express'. One difference between the two railways to the casual observer was the comfort factor – Midland carriages having more comfortable and roomier seats than the GWR! The Midland was also noted for the quality of its restaurant cars.

Speed became of increasing importance during the 1920s and 1930s – the GWR introduced the 'Cheltenham Flyer' which for some years did not call at Gloucester station, instead taking the loop line, with a coach from Hereford and Ross-on-Wye being attached at Gloucester South. Meanwhile the LMS accelerated its services in the area – Bristol to Gloucester, 37 miles, was regularly scheduled in 43 minutes after trials were conducted in 1937 from Bristol to Birmingham and the north with 'Jubilee' locomotive 5660 *Rooke* of Bristol shed, leading to faster trains. One of these was the 'Devonian' from Bradford to Bristol and, in the summer, through to Paignton, which became a good fast service between Birmingham and Gloucester, 63 minutes with a stop at Cheltenham. This train was originally introduced in 1927, with through carriages for Paignton being added to a GWR train at Bristol outside the summer season.

The railways had always promoted excursion trains, not just to the seaside, but also for sporting events – rugby and cricket matches at Gloucester – or visits to the Cathedral, with cheap fares from outlying stations on the main and branch lines. Special excursion trains were also run from branch stations such as Dursley and Nailsworth. The GWR was keen on inclusive days out, an example being a train from the London area down to Gloucester for a road trip through the Wye Valley. With the introduction of paid holidays, there was a huge upsurge in workers having a week at the seaside, with resorts in the West Country and south coast being obvious attractions for families from Birmingham and the industrial Midlands. Naturally many extra trains on both the GWR and LMS flowed through Gloucester to cater for this traffic in the summer, peaking around the end of July and early August and including a good number of overnight workings.

1939 and wartime brought a halt to those balmy days, with an emergency timetable introduced, but the trains which still ran were, more often than not, impossibly crowded. Heavy usage and lack of routine maintenance during the War meant services were slow to recover their 1930s timings in the post-war period, so Nationalisation in 1948 did not have any great immediate effect. A portent of things to come was the 'temporary' cessation of passenger trains on the lines from Stonehouse to Stroud and Nailsworth, on and from 16 June 1947; this was made permanent on and from 8 June 1949.

BR introduced the Mark 1 coach in 1951 and these began to appear on trains in the area. In 1956 the Western Region used the GWR livery of chocolate and cream for Mark 1s on certain services, including the newly re-introduced 'Cheltenham Spa Express' – though a rather slower service than its pre-war counterpart – and the 'Cornishman' from Wolverhampton to Penzance, which first ran on the route in 1952.

Holiday traffic in the 1950s was extremely busy, and, on Summer Saturdays, Gloucester was often clogged up with passenger trains on all lines, particularly with northbound workings in the early to mid afternoon.

Modernisation arrived in the form of diesel multiple units which gradually took over a number of local services in the Gloucester area on ex-GWR lines, as well as the express workings from Birmingham Snow Hill to South Wales – which had been operated by GWR railcars during the 1930s. The railcars had been a familiar part of the scene for years, often being used on Cinderford and Ledbury trains as well as some other turns including the Cheltenham service.

Local rail travel was in decline, however, and there were cutbacks well before the Beeching era of closures – passenger trains from Gloucester to Cinderford ceased on and from 3 November 1958, with stations and halts on the branch from Bullo shutting down. The service from Gloucester to Ledbury ceased on and from 13 July 1959.

The Lydney to Berkeley Road working across the Severn Bridge was abruptly curtailed in October 1960, when a tanker sailing up the river hit the bridge. After that it ran from Berkeley Road to Sharpness only. The exception was the service for schoolchildren which continued, but taking the long way round – via Gloucester, adding considerably to the journey time.

Moving into the 1960s, main line diesel locomotives became more prominent – Western Region diesel hydraulics on some London trains, and Midland Region diesel electrics on selected cross-country trains from June 1961 – the latter also being based at Bristol for expresses to Birmingham New Street and the north. Hydraulics also sometimes appeared on summer Saturday holiday trains from the West Midlands.

September 1962 wrought more cutbacks for steam, with the 'Pines Express' being diverted and no longer appearing at Gloucester, while the 'Cornishman' had its routing altered and was now diesel hauled. Horton Road's 'Castle' locos, so immaculately turned out over the years, officially lost their London workings to diesels. Branch cutbacks became more pronounced – Dursley to Coaley Junction passengers, and the daily mixed, stopped running on 8 September 1962, again pre-Beeching. But the Beeching axe was swung vigorously on 31 October 1964, with a wholesale slaughter of local steam-hauled services,

Above: The GWR station had two main platform faces with crossovers enabling more than one train to occupy them. On 12 August 1959 large Prairie tank 4115 of Hereford shed is at the down platform on a local passenger train while an 0-6-0PT stands further along with two auto coaches. There were also up and down bays, with part of the latter visible on the right.
Sid Rickard, B J Miller collection

Below: 'Jubilee' 45651 *Shovell* is on the up 'Devonian' at Eastgate on 20 June 1953. The loco and crew would work through to Leeds. The up and down trains were diagrammed for 'Jubilees' from Bristol Barrow Road and Leeds Holbeck which were, generally speaking, kept nice and clean. In the late 1920s and 1930s there were occasions when the down 'Devonian' was worked by a GWR engine from Gloucester, though this is not thought to have occurred in BR steam days.
B W L Brooksbank, Initial Photographics

including Gloucester to Hereford; Berkeley Road to Sharpness; and perhaps the deepest cut of all, the Chalford autos. Also from 2 November 1964, Cheltenham to London trains started using Eastgate station, doing away with reversal at Central and the need to change engines, enabling diesel locos to work throughout. These changes made a lot of Gloucester-based steam engines redundant. From 4 January 1965, many intermediate stations on the ex-Midland Bristol-Birmingham line were closed and, while the stopping train service on the route was reduced, some remained steam for a few more months. Apart from the very occasional sighting of a steam loco on a passenger or empty stock working, the end was in sight by December 1965, with just one passenger train normally still steam, the 5pm Gloucester Central to Cheltenham St. James, utilising whatever loco was available. After closure of St. James on 1 January 1966, the service was transferred to Cheltenham's Lansdown station, and managed to be steam-hauled a few times that month, by a 'Black Five' 4-6-0. The same class regularly worked a night parcels from and to Birmingham via the Honeybourne line as far as Gloucester until this, too, succumbed to diesel operation at the beginning of August 1966, while further implementation of the National Freight Train Plan at this date virtually eliminated all steam workings to Gloucester.

LOCOMOTIVES

The Birmingham & Gloucester Railway had 21 loco-motives in November 1840 when public services first ran at Gloucester: three were 2-2-2s; one 0-4-0; one 0-4-2; and the rest were 4-2-0s, mostly of the famous Norris design, considered by management to be the most suitable type of engine for working the Lickey Incline between Broms-grove and Blackwell. Loco 10, a Norris, was named *Gloucester*. Further locos were acquired in later years.

When the broad gauge Bristol & Gloucester Railway arrived in July 1844, it had five 2-2-2s and one 0-6-0, all built by Stothert & Slaughter in Bristol, who were also contracted to work the line. Loco 5, a 2-2-2, was also named *Gloucester*.

The two railways formed a joint board of management in January 1845 and purchased more locos, including secondhand ones. 39 standard gauge and 11 broad gauge locos were allocated Midland Railway numbers in February 1847. A few of the early engines had been rebuilt as saddle tanks in Birmingham & Gloucester days, while some were used by the MR only as stationary boilers.

Following extension of standard gauge services to Bristol on 1 June 1854, the serviceable broad gauge locos were gradually sold off to contractor Thomas Brassey for the North Devon Railway.

The Midland Railway's own locomotives were mostly 2-2-2s, 2-4-0s and 0-6-0s, built by a variety of private builders and in the railway's Derby Works from the early 1850s.

Meanwhile the Great Western Railway's broad gauge engines in those early days were mainly 2-2-2s and 0-6-0s. A notable event at Gloucester station yard on 7 February 1855 was a boiler explosion on a 'Firefly' class 2-2-2, due to shortage of water. A class of ten 4-4-0s, the 'Waverley' class, built not by Swindon Works, but by Robert Stephenson & Co, were used between Swindon and South Wales from the mid-1850s. It was one of these, *Rob Roy*, which was involved in a fatal collision at Bullo Pill in November 1868. A photograph of a gauge conversion train at Grange Court in 1869 shows a broad gauge 0-6-0 with open cab. Broad gauge 4-4-0ST were photographed at Gloucester, while locos of the 2-4-0 wheel arrangement were probably common.

After May 1872 all locomotives working at Gloucester were standard gauge. The GWR shed had a couple of 7' Singles, 1122 and 1123, for some years to haul expresses through to London, returning with the 5.45pm Milford boat express. These engines were transferred to Swindon in 1887 and replaced at Horton Road by 6'6" Singles 73 and 76, which were familiar in the area as they already worked from Swindon as far as Neath. After allocation to Gloucester they also worked to Hereford. E L Ahrons wrote that the class did 'some wonderful climbing' up the 'continuous series of sharp S curves' on Sapperton 'with trains up to about 130 tons' without the assistance of a banker. An interesting loco used on the Swindon-Gloucester line in 1886/7 was a four cylinder compound double-frame 2-4-0, number 7. It worked slow trains to and from Cardiff, and Ahrons notes that the coupling rod pins struck sparks off the coping stones on one or two platforms on the line. Other 2-4-0 tender types had quite long careers in the area, while Gloucester shed had 2-4-0T for working slow passenger trains to Cardiff. Double-framed 0-6-0ST, double-headed, featured on the process-ion of heavy coal trains from Aberdare via Gloucester to Swindon. 0-6-0ST were also busy shunting and doing trip work, and local passengers if required, though these were generally headed by 0-4-2T and 2-4-0T.

Over on the Midland, expresses were worked by Singles and 2-4-0s, with freights being the province of 0-6-0s. Some passenger trains, like Gloucester to Lydney via Berkeley Road and the Severn Bridge were worked by 0-4-4Ts, as were passengers on the Stroud and Nailsworth branches. The Dursley branch seemed to be an exception for many years, being worked by 0-6-0T. If they were not available 0-6-0 tender engines were used. The Midland gradually introduced inside cylinder 4-4-0s on its expresses, many of which were double-headed, the pilot

15

Above: The former Midland Railway roundhouse at Barnwood was opened in July 1894 to replace the depot which was demolished to make way for the new station, called Gloucester Eastgate in BR days. Barnwood shed yard often had at least one loco with a set of wheels removed awaiting repair after getting a hot box and on 27 September 1953 it is a relatively new BR Standard class 5 4-6-0. After closure in May 1964, the remaining working engines and crews transferred to Horton Road shed.   *Brian Hilton*

being a Single or 2-4-0. The docks at Gloucester on the MR side were mainly worked by various types of 0-4-0ST due to the sharp curvatures encountered there.

Trains had become heavier by the start of the 1900s and new motive power was required. The GWR started building 4-4-0s in the 1890s and this type worked services through Gloucester including the new Birmingham-Bristol trains. Dean double-framed 'Aberdare' 2-6-0s were introduced on goods trains, while Churchward's new 2-8-0s were even more revolutionary. Prairie tanks, with the 2-6-2 wheel arrangement, came onto the scene and one local duty was the Brimscombe banker. The GWR had a brief flirtation with Atlantics, 4-4-2, which got to Gloucester, but settled on 4-6-0s as its main type for many passenger, parcel and express freight duties, with 'Saint' and 'Star' classes soon becoming daily features. The Churchward 2-6-0 Moguls also came out of Swindon Works and established themselves as motive power for just about any duty – stopping passenger and freight on both main lines and branches as well as being capable power for relief expresses and holiday traffic.

Gloucester Horton Road was not one of the GWR's top

sheds, so tended to have to still perform its own diagrammed duties with older engines.

The same applied to the MR shed at Barnwood. Larger 4-4-0s, class 3, appeared on the top trains, but none were allocated to Gloucester, which made do with the smaller 4-4-0s. In MR days, Gloucester was often a loco changing point on through trains, less so in the LMS period. The last two working 4-2-2 Singles on the LMS, 673 (preserved today, numbered 118) and 679, were at Gloucester, entrusted with locals to Bristol or the light afternoon express to Bath until withdrawal in 1928. Kirtley double-framed 2-4-0s were still around at that time, as were the Kirtley double-framed 0-4-4T. 0-6-0T did a lot of yard shunting and local trip work. Compound 4-4-0s did not appear until the mid-1920s – 1000 (now preserved), 1001 and 1002 were just some of the type on Barnwood's allocation in LMS days. A couple of fast Compound turns in the early 1930s were the eight-coach 10.25am and 2.25pm expresses from Bristol, timed to cover the Mangotsfield to Gloucester section, 31.9 miles, in 31 minutes. Horwich Moguls were new on the scene in the 1920s and did quite a lot of work, including express passenger and fast freights such as the Burton beer trains. The Fowler 4F 0-6-0 was first built in 1911, but Barnwood did not get any representatives until the 1920s, with 4045 and 4046, possibly from when they were new in 1925. 4045 spent virtually its whole life at Gloucester. Other post-grouping changes saw double-framed 0-6-0s from the Somerset & Dorset Railway working on the Stroud and Nailsworth branches, before they gave way to Lancashire & Yorkshire Railway 0-6-0s. In 1926, two ex London & North Western Railway 4-4-0s of the 'Renown' class worked a daily Birmingham to Gloucester local. Apparently a Fowler short wheelbase 0-6-0 dock tank, 7160, was tried at Gloucester.

An interesting development took place in 1928 when the 'Devonian' on Saturdays, and, later, Fridays as well, changed from an LMS to a GWR engine at Gloucester – hitherto this had been done at Bristol. So there was the sight of a 'Saint' going up Tuffley Bank. This arrangement lasted until 1939, with the 'Hall', 'Star' and 'Castle' class all being involved.

In the mid-1930s, Horton Road had three 'Saint' and two of the new 'Hall' 4-6-0s on its roster, but no 'Star' or 'Castle' class, though these appeared everyday from other sheds. It also housed some of the former Midland & South Western Junction 0-6-0s and 4-4-0s, formerly used from Cheltenham to Southampton – these had all gone before the World War 2. On the LMS, the 'Patriot' or 'Baby Scot' 3-cylinder 4-6-0s began to come through on expresses, then the 3-cylinder 'Jubilee' 4-6-0s and the new Stanier mixed traffic 4-6-0s, popularly known as 'Black Fives'. Two or three of the latter were allocated from new to Barnwood for a while. On the freight side, Fowler 4F 0-6-0s were now very common and Stanier 8F 2-8-0s were also seen. Gloucester based 4Fs, and also 3Fs, were frequently used on excursion traffic, the former certainly working as far as Blackpool, with a Barnwood crew. Facilities at Barnwood for attending to hot boxes on engines meant ex-Somerset & Dorset 2-8-0s and the famous Lickey Banker 0-10-0 22290 'Big Bertha' were sometimes seen at Gloucester.

Another noteworthy addition to the scene in the mid-

Above: Horton Road, the ex-Great Western loco shed, is depicted in this view taken in 1960/61. The shed had been opened in 1872. In 1921 improvements were made including a new coal stage built to replace a hoist. In mid-1947, coded GLO, it had an allocation of 63 locos plus a diesel railcar. At that date, there were also 20 locos allocated to the sub-shed of Lydney, LYD, with another 16 at Cheltenham, CHEL; these all came under one BR code, 85B, which had an allocation of over 90 locos in the mid-1950s. It continued to see steam activity into 1966, some months after the official end of steam on the Western Region.

B J Miller collection

1930s was the GWR railcar type, which had a daily express from Birmingham to Cardiff as well as appearances on local trains. An LMS 3-car diesel set also showed up in March 1938 on a trial run.

During World War 2, some fairly ancient Southern 4-4-0s and London North Eastern Railway 0-6-0s were on loan at Gloucester for shunting and local trip work. New 2-8-0 locomotives built in the USA were on loan to the railways in the war and were regularly seen in and around Gloucester, as were the home built War Department 2-8-0s of the Ministry of Supply, many of which passed into BR ownership.

With nationalisation in 1948, the two sheds and indeed the two railways continued to function separately as if the change had not happened. At this time, Horton Road had three 'Castles' on its allocation. A new type passing through was the Ivatt class 4 2-6-0, introduced in 1947, with some shedded at Bath and Bristol. A rebuilt 'Royal Scot' 4-6-0, 46120, made some trial runs from Derby in February 1949.

The 1950s witnessed the introduction of BR Standard types and with some being constructed at Swindon Works they were run-in on local passenger trains to Gloucester – the likes of the 77000 2-6-0s class were otherwise not seen in the area. 'Britannia' Pacifics were allocated to the Western Region and often had Gloucester-Paddington trains. On the other side of the coin, engines from South Wales going to Swindon for scrap were also seen being towed through Gloucester, as they were not allowed through the Severn Tunnel. Round about November 1954, a new 9F 2-10-0 was spotted at Gloucester and this ultimate BR freight engine type came through increasingly, causing something of a sensation in Summer 1957 by working long-distance passenger trains on Saturdays – the class continued on these passenger duties until at least 1964, despite the availability of main line diesels by then. It was also not uncommon to see LMS Beyer-Garratt 2-6-2/2-6-2s into the mid-1950s going through to Westerleigh on coal trains – these engines often came back light to Gloucester to turn and be serviced. Ex-LNWR 0-8-0 freight engines also put in appearances, not only from Birmingham and the north, but also off the Hereford line.

When Barnwood was finally completely transferred to Western Region control in February 1958, changing from shed code 22B to 85E (85C from January 1961) it was not long before the ubiquitous GWR 0-6-0PT appeared on the allocation to do duties like the Ashchurch-Upton-on-Severn branch. Similar boundary changes between the London Midland and Eastern Regions at Sheffield led to ex-LNER B1 4-6-0s being seen with increasing frequency on various through workings. The effects of dieselisation on BR also led to regular workings by 'Royal Scot' 4-6-0 based at sheds like Derby and Saltley.

Further into the 1960s and the final years of steam at Gloucester saw 'Castles' on relief and Summer Saturday passengers, rather than the daily expresses, also on locals which had formerly been Moguls or 2-6-2T. And, whisper it not, even on ballast and works trains, such as 4093 *Dunster Castle* turned out by Horton Road on 29 August 1964 for one of these duties. 'Jubilees' worked the Burton beer and lesser freight trains, while freight sheds like Annesley inherited 'Royal Scots' and 'Britannias', sometimes seen at Gloucester on relief passenger, local

Gloucester GWR shed (GLO) – allocation at 31 December 1947				
0-4-2T	1406	1413	1424	1464	
0-6-0PT	1943	1989	2009	2146	2756
0-6-0PT	3609	4627	4628	4659	5793
0-6-0PT	7723	7741	8701	8717	8731
0-6-0PT	8781	9727	9776		
0-6-0	2248	3204	3205	3213	
2-6-0	2656	5312	5336	5347	5394
2-6-0	5398	6309	6381		
4-6-0	2938	2980	4059	4082	
4-6-0	4977	5042	5951	5965	5980
4-6-0	5988	5990	6917	6940	7004
4-6-0	7815				
2-6-2T	3153	3164	3171	3175	4140
2-6-2T	4534				
4-4-0	3379	9064	9089		
0-6-2T	5697	6623	6681		
2-8-0	90179	90413	90691	90715	
Railcar	25				

Gloucester LMS shed (22B) – allocation at 31 December 1947				
4-4-0	437	523	530	1001	1019
4-4-0	1025	1027	1039	1058	1074
4-4-0	1097				
0-4-0T	1530	1537			
0-6-0T	1720	1727	1870		
2-6-0	2922				
0-6-0	3062	3213	3257	3258	3263
0-6-0	3344	3373	3427	3506	3507
0-6-0	3604	3645	3754	3791	3846
0-6-0	3887	3924	3932	3978	4045
0-6-0	4167	4175	4229	4235	4269
0-6-0	4272	4553	4576		
0-6-0T	7237	7619	7620	7635	
0-4-4T	1251	1303	1353	1365	

Lydney GWR shed (LYD) – allocation at 31 December 1947				
0-4-2T	1409	1441	1456		
0-6-0PT	2025	2034	2039	2043	2044
0-6-0PT	2045	2080	2091	2102	2114
0-6-0PT	2121	2131	2132	2144	2153
0-6-0PT	2155	2160			
0-6-0	2350	2515			

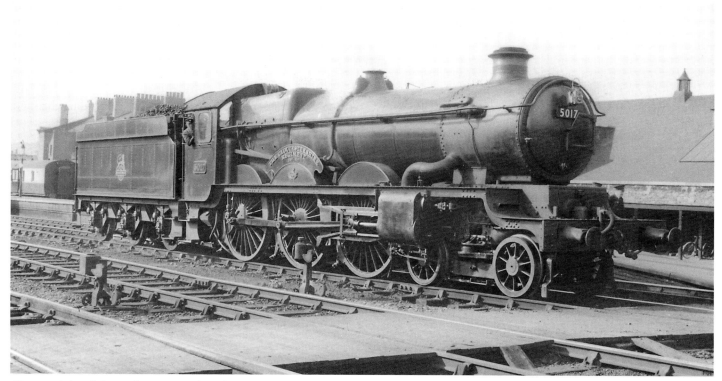

Above: A local favourite, 5017 *The Gloucestershire Regiment 28th,61st* is depicted at the west end of Central station on 12 May 1956. Horton Road's small stud of 'Castles' had a good reputation for running and cleanliness. When 5017 was transferred to Gloucester from Worcester in November 1951, it was called *St. Donats Castle*; the renaming to *The Gloucestershire Regiment 28th,61st* took place in the down bay at Gloucester Central station on 24 April 1954 with various dignitaries in attendance. A nice touch was that the footplate crew were both ex-Gloucestershire Regiment men. It is also worth recalling that the change of name was approved after being suggested by the Gloucestershire Railway Society, to commemorate the County regiment and its heroic exploits during the Korean War, which were still very fresh in people's minds.   *G W Sharpe*

trains and parcels duties.

As lines shut and services contracted, Barnwood shed closed in May 1964, with its remaining staff and engines, including 4Fs, transferring to Horton Road. For a while, this made Horton Road overcrowded, so Barnwood still saw some working locos. But it became a repository for condemned engines and wagons on their way to scrap yards. Horton Road also had lines of redundant engines, particularly after the cuts at the end of October 1964. With the official end of Western Region steam at Gloucester on and from 3 January 1966, that might have been it, but steam continued to appear from the London Midland Region. While ex-GWR types had finished in the area covered by this book, ex-LMS and BR Standard locos could still be seen on lines from Birmingham and working into South Wales, as well as Bristol and Swindon. There was fresh loco coal delivered to Horton Road in 1966. Preserved 'Manor' class 4-6-0 7808 *Cookham Manor* was still at Horton Road when it did a steam test run on 14 July 1966 from Gloucester to Honeybourne and back. With some sheds like Saltley having steam facilities available until March 1967, working steam into Gloucester was still possible, but after September 1966, it was rarely reported.

It has not been possible in this brief survey to mention every class seen in the area, suffice to say that just about every engine type was allowed, from all BR regions, apart from the very largest, class 8 passenger engines. But, having said that, there was the 'King' 6018 *King Henry VI* which got to Gloucester when it should not have done, on a train from South Wales. It was promptly removed and sent light engine to Bristol. Another GW class thought of as very rare at Gloucester was the big 4700 2-8-0 type. However, the class was actually officially diagrammed in 1957 for a late night Sundays only freight from Llandilo to London, and, indeed, 4705 was seen leaving Central early one Monday in August that year. Other notable sightings include V2 2-6-2s a couple of times in late 1959 on trains from the north-east and 'Clan' 4-6-2 72005 *Clan Macgregor* on 9 July 1960 with an overnight relief passenger, which it worked to Bristol. And Southern Region light Pacifics may have appeared more often than generally realised, on a night freight from Westerleigh, and not just on the two occasions in December 1960 when the up 'Pines Express' was diverted due to a landslip on the Somerset & Dorset line, causing the rostered loco to work through to Gloucester, and, once, to Birmingham New Street.

Churchdown to Engine Shed Junction

Left: One of the more rambling cross-country workings during the inter-war period was the 11.30am Gloucester to Lowestoft. The train, depicted in this shot of 'Crab' 2824 north of Churchdown in 1939, ran via Birmingham, Leicester, the Midland & Great Northern Joint line, Norwich and Yarmouth. In an earlier era, it was also possible to book with the GWR from Gloucester to East Anglia, which in summer 1908 introduced a short-lived service from Cardiff to Yarmouth and Lowestoft via Gloucester, Leamington and Peterborough. *LGRP*

Above: A delightful portrait of the Edwardian era at Churchdown station as a GWR train coasts in from Cheltenham. In 1914 the GWR had sixteen local trains stopping on the way from Cheltenham to Gloucester, whilst the Midland Railway had only four at this joint station. Churchdown did not have any sidings so heavy traffic like coal had to be carted by road from Gloucester. In July 1942 up and down goods lines were added around the outside of the platforms. But it was March 1944 before the latter were altered to accomodate stopping passenger trains, after which the goods lines were termed relief lines.

Left: The signal box at the new station dates from the 1942 alterations. Compound 41049 has the 2.45pm Worcester to Bristol local on 3 August 1957, which stopped at every station *en route* – except Churchdown.
B W L Brooksbank

Right, above: On 4 November 1961, the 11.45am Cheltenham to Paddington express passes the new station without stopping. Motive power is ex-works loco 3201 of 'rare' shed 89B Croes Newydd (Wrexham), presumably running-in and borrowed by Gloucester. The up and down platforms and the modest buildings can be seen, but the loco's exhaust has blotted out the signal box.   *B W L Brooksbank*

Right, below: On Summer Saturday afternoons in the 1950s, even with two northbound tracks available, trains were often 'on the block' between Gloucester and Cheltenham, such was the volume of holiday traffic heading back home after a week or two at the seaside. Trains heading north tended to be concentrated into Saturday afternoon while southbound ones started coming down on Friday night and continued through the early hours until Saturday lunchtime. Train 873, the 11.15am Newquay-Wolverhampton, approaches Churchdown on 9 August 1958 behind 5912 *Queen's Hall* and a rake of Southern Region carriages. This train was routed via Gloucester South and the Honeybourne line from Cheltenham.   *B W L Brooksbank*

Below: Stanier 'Black Five' 4812 heads through Churchdown for Gloucester on the down main with a parcels train on 13 April 1946. Two tracks were added here in 1942 as part of the substantial work done to increase the number of running lines between Cheltenham Lansdown Junction and Gloucester Engine Shed Junction. The new layout lasted until 1966/67 when the route reverted to two tracks.   *E R Morten*

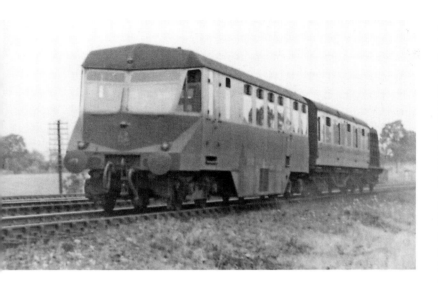

Left, above: GWR railcar 25 is on its way to Gloucester from Cheltenham St James in July 1949 towing a carriage and a gas oil tank wagon. A number of the frequent services between these two neighbouring places were worked by railcars. Gloucester usually had at least one allocated, sometimes two; W19W and W20W stick in the author's mind, but there were others at various times, including W25W. The first GWR diesel railcar express service was inaugurated on 9 July 1934 between Birmingham Snow Hill, Gloucester, Newport and Cardiff. *W Dendy*

Left, below: Royal Scot' 46118 *Royal Welch Fusilier* heads 1N46, the 8.40am Bournemouth-Bradford, due away from Eastgate at 12.29pm, along the up relief line at Elm Bridge. This train ran for a short period on Saturdays only from 15 July to 26 August 1961. In the early 1960s it was not uncommon to see half a dozen or more 'Royal Scot' and rebuilt 'Patriot' 4-6-0s in a day, whereas they had been relatively rare in the area in the 1950s. Their displacement on the West Coast main line by diesels handed them transfers to depots such as Derby and Saltley. *Author's collection*

Below: The last of its class in service, 1011 *County of Chester*, heads a Stephenson Locomotive Society special on the way from Worcester to Swindon at Engine Shed Junction on 20 September 1964. The train is coming off the down main and heading for Gloucester South, so avoiding the stations. Participants on the tour, including the author, were able to visit both Worcester and Swindon Works. It was a strange time at the latter, with non-GWR locos such as LNER V2 2-6-2s being present for scrapping and Stanier and Ivatt 2-6-0s in works for overhaul. *John Goss*

Above: On 8 August 1964 0-6-0PT 9606 heads a Cheltenham-bound local past Barnwood on the part of the triangle between Tramway Junction and Engine Shed Junction. All the signals are upper quadrants. The buildings in the left background are in the Engineers Yard, while the chimney glimpsed on the right is at Barnwood loco shed, officially closed by this date, but being used for wagon storage and staging of withdrawn locos on their way to scrap yards.

R K Blencowe collection

Barnwood locomotive depot

Below: The approach to the roundhouse is shown in May 1958, with a gathering of fine motor cars on display – though most employees here would still be walking or using a bicycle to get to and from work. *J Bateman*

Left: Three Barnwood locos, all ex-Midland Railway, are depicted in the roundhouse on 11 April 1954 – condenser fitted 1P 0-4-4 passenger tank 58071, flanked by 3F 0-6-0s 43258 and 43373. 58071 usually worked the Ashchurch to Upton-on-Severn line up to withdrawal in June 1956; it was fitted with round top firebox and Salter safety valves until its demise. 43258 has the front buffer plank removed for work on valves and pistons. *T J Edgington collection*

Left, below: 4-4-0s of various power classifications were the Midland Railway's standard passenger engines. 2P 40423 seen posing in the yard was constructed in 1918, as part of the '483' class, which was employed on express train haulage through Gloucester for many years. 40423 transferred to Barnwood in 1951 from Bristol Barrow Road, but did not last long, being withdrawn in August 1952. Obviously Barrow Road did not want to give away its best engines! It was replaced by 40540, remembered by many as one of the last two Midland 4-4-0s at Barnwood, along with 40537. 40540 was not withdrawn until February 1962 although it had been in store for some while. *Author's collection*

Below: 0-6-0s were the Midland Railway's standard goods engines. This one, 3062, has a modest claim to fame, in being the last Midland 2F to receive its BR number, 58206, in June 1953. Built by Robert Stephenson & Co in 1880, it was Midland Railway 1444, part of the '1357' Express Goods class. Rebuilt in 1899, 1913 and again in 1926, the loco was renumbered 3062 in 1907. A Gloucester engine for over 20 years, in latter days it was the 'Ballast Engine' on Civil Engineer's duties – the author often saw it dashing home through Cheltenham with a brake van and a few wagons. 3062 also has vacuum brakes and carriage warming apparatus, so could perform other duties. After withdrawal in July 1957, another 2F, 58165, came as a replacement, staying until December 1958, when it went elsewhere for further work. *Author's collection*

Above: Various four-coupled tank locos shunted the Midland side of Gloucester Docks over the years. Deeley 0-4-0Ts were in charge during BR steam days and 41530, 41535 and 41537 all did lengthy stints at the docks. The usual allocation was two at a time – one at work and one spare. However, this portrait in the roundhouse depicts 41533 during the period of about a year from July 1951, when it was allocated here along with 41530 and 41537, making three in total – out of a class of just ten engines! 41533 was probably deputising for 41537 which was in Derby Works for a time.   *Author's collection*

Below: While Johnson 0-4-4Ts were the archetypal Midland branch passenger locos, 0-6-0Ts were entrusted with Coaley Junction to Dursley trains and one of the regular engines in the early to mid-1950s was half cab Johnson Class 1F 41748. It was transferred to Barnwood in March 1952, still with 'LMS' on the tanks, being a direct replacement for the full cab 41727 which was withdrawn the same month, and shared the work with classmate 41720, also a half cab. In this picture 41748 has a fifty year old round-top boiler with Salter safety valves, but January 1953 saw it in Derby Works having a replacement Belpaire boiler fitted. In 1956 / 57 these old Midland engines were ousted by the Great Western type, but BR built, 1600 class 0-6-0PT. Stanier 0-4-4T 41900 had an apparently unsuccessful trial on the line around the end of February 1957; its usual duty while shedded at Gloucester was working Ashchurch to Upton-on-Severn trains.   *Author's collection*

Above: Barnwood's own 0-6-0T 47417 stands outside the old fitting shop. 47417 came to Gloucester in December 1955 because a vacuum fitted shunting loco was required for various duties at Cheltenham. It is still so fitted in this undated picture; it has an 85E shed plate so is sometime after February 1958 but before January 1961 when the code changed to 85C. Note the set of driving wheels in the wagon, doubtless off a loco which got a hot box and is at Barnwood for repair. The wheels would be shipped to a main Works for attention – usually Derby, Crewe, Horwich or Swindon depending on the type of loco.   *Author's collection*

Below: Beyer-Garratt 47994 occupies the coal stage on 7 July 1956. During the early to mid-1950s the type was seen at Gloucester on freights from the north to Westerleigh and also to Over Sidings, before coming to Barnwood depot for servicing. They were perhaps never as successful as the LMS and their builders, Beyer Peacock, would have liked, despite the undoubted benefits the Garratt design had brought to various railways abroad. As BR 9F 2-10-0s were introduced into traffic from the mid-1950s, the Garratts were taken out of service and 47994 was the last of the class to be officially withdrawn, in April 1958.   *Author's collection*

Right: 'Jubilee' 4-6-0 45598 *Basutoland* has arrived at the shed for servicing on Sunday 30 June 1963 after bringing special passenger train 1X36 down to Gloucester. It is allocated to Burton, 17B, which found itself with quite a number of the class following dieselisation of traditional 'Jubilee' turns at other depots. They became regulars on the Burton beer trains for a while, displacing 'Crab' 2-6-0s.

Joe Moss collection, R S Carpenter

Below: The Midland Railway and LMS built a total of eleven Fowler 2-8-0s for service between Bath and Bournemouth over the Somerset & Dorset Railway – though never perpetuated the design for use elsewhere. The type appeared at Gloucester on freight or en route to Derby Works for overhaul, but there was an occasion in the 1950s when 53800 came up from Bath on the 'Pines Express' or one of its relief trains double-headed with S&D based 4-4-0 40700. 53807 is at Barnwood for repair, probably to a hot box; a set of driving wheels has been removed and sent to Derby Works for attention. Locos from the former Midland depots at Bristol and Bath were regularly stopped at Gloucester for such repairs, as neither of those places had a wheel drop. GW locos could also be found having attention here. After repair, locos were often run-in on a local turn, like working a trip to the docks. 53806 did so in May 1961 – despite the class not being authorised on the High Orchard line!

Author's collection

Gloucester Triangle and Tramway Junction

On summer Saturdays quite a number of holiday relief trains took the avoiding line between Gloucester South and Engine Shed Junction. These two workings were also on 8 August 1964 – 5056 Earl of Powis heads 1V54, 10.5am Wolverhampton to Kingswear, due past Engine Shed Junction at 12.15pm, having stopped at Cheltenham. Malvern Road. Later the same day 9F 92125 has 1N40, 10.20am Newton Abbot to Bradford, which was scheduled to stop at Gloucester South for water at 2pm. Built for heavy freight haulage, BR 9F 2-10-0s proved equally adept at running passenger trains should the need arise – which it certainly did on summer Saturdays, when the motive power department was hard pressed to find enough engines to work the busy holiday traffic of the 1950s and early 1960s. Although the regular long-distance passenger workings were pretty well dieselised by 1964, many of the dated summer reliefs were still steam. Other 'Castles' and 9Fs noted on similar duties this day were 4082, 5026, 5063, 7023, 92000 and 92160. *R K Blencowe collection*

Left: Pannier tank 3693 is at the head of a transfer trip for New Yard, with wagons picked up at various places for marshalling into main line freights. Notice the two brake vans in the centre of the train. The brake van which can be seen to the right of the loco is in the Engineers Yard. On the far left of the picture is a signal on the passenger lines between Gloucester South and North. In 1957 New Yard had two shunting locos – one Front Road and one Back Road, both for 144 hours a week, with a change of engine during the day. Other locos did trip workings from the 'T' Sidings, which was part of the New Yard complex.

Restoration and Archiving Trust

Some Western Region freight trains starting and terminating at Gloucester in 1957, and diagrammed locomotives.

DEPARTURES

Train	Headcode	From	To	Loco
1.50am MX	H	T Sidings	Swindon	43XX
5.10am	H	T Sidings	Hereford	57XX
10.10am	K	Docks Branch Sidings	Severn Tunnel Jc	56XX
10.20am	K	T Sidings	Swindon	49XX
4.32pm	H	T Sidings	Severn Tunnel Jc	56XX
6.30pm SO	D	Old Yard	Paddington	49XX
6.35pm	F	Docks Branch Sidings	Woodford Halse	WD 2-8-0
6.35pm	H	Old Yard	Hereford	22XX
7.50pm	E	Docks Branch Sidings	Llandilo Jc	28XX
8.40pm SX	D	T Sidings	Old Oak Common	49XX
9.10pm	H	T Sidings	Swindon	56XX
9.45pm	H	T Sidings	Stoke Gifford	43XX
11.20pm SO	E	T Sidings	Cardiff	49XX
11.30pm Su	H	T Sidings	Hanwell Bridge	49XX

ARRIVALS

Train	Headcode	From	To	Loco
12.15am	H	Rogerstone	Over	WD 2-8-0
2.0am	F	Rogerstone	Docks Branch Sidings	43XX
3.10am	F	Cardiff	Barnwood	49XX
8.5am	K	Severn Tunnel Jc	Old Yard	56XX
10.35am	H	Cardiff	Over	43XX
4.35pm	F	Hereford	Gloucester	43XX
7.35pm	H	Hereford	Gloucester	57XX
9.45pm	H	Llandilo Jc	Over	28XX

Some Western Region freight trains travelling through Gloucester in 1957

Train	Headcode	From	To	Loco
4.10am	F	Margam	Banbury	28XX
8.20am SX	H	Cardiff	Yarnton	28XX
9.45am	H	Alexandra Dock Jc	Stourbridge	28XX
11.55am	H	Cheltenham High St	Newport	43XX
1.0pm	H	Severn Tunnel Jc	Moreton Cutting	BR Std 5
4.45pm SX	H	Aberdare	Old Oak Common	28XX
10.0pm Su	H	Llandilo Jc	Hanwell Bridge	47XX
11.15pm	D	Cardiff	Bordesley	49XX
11.50pm SX	D	Llandilo Jc	Old Oak Common	68XX

Above: Collett 0-6-0 2203 of Swindon shed approaches Tramway as it drags a long train of mineral wagons off the goods line at New Yard on 25 May 1956. Part of the line to Engine Shed Junction and Cheltenham is visible on the left and to Tuffley, Standish Junction and Swindon on the right. The tall signal post on the right is a Midland Railway one, with LMS arms – on a GWR line!
R K Blencowe collection

Left, above: A typical auto train – a 1400 class 0-4-2T and one coach – makes its way out of Gloucester bound for all stations and halts to Chalford. These workings provided a vital service for people living in the Stroud valley and it was a bad day indeed when they ran for the last time on 31 October 1964. At least there are still stations at Stonehouse and Stroud. The end of Barnwood yard can just be seen through the loco's exhaust, as can the line from Cheltenham.

Left, below: The 'Cornishman' to Penzance arrives at Tramway behind 7026 *Tenby Castle* on Saturday 16 June 1962, signalled as usual into Eastgate station, where it was due just after 11am. From the following Saturday, 23 June, the 'Cornishman' lost its name, being just another train, though retaining it from Monday to Friday. The train came from Wolver-hampton via Birmingham Snow Hill and Stratford-upon-Avon until 10 September 1962 when it started at Sheffield and traversed the old Midland Railway route from Birmingham, through Bromsgrove – and was diagrammed for diesel power.
B W L Brooksbank, Initial Photographics

Right: Tramway Junction signal box alongside Horton Road level crossing was extremely busy at all hours, being in a pivotal location. The box depicted dated from May 1927, replacing an earlier one on the same site. It was extended in the Second World War and survived until the Gloucester area power box, on the opposite side of the lines, was brought into use in late May 1968. The new system heralded the closure of this and many other boxes in the area including Engine Shed Junction, Gloucester South and Gloucester North. And Tramway Junction was renamed Horton Road Junction.

R K Blencowe collection

Below: 0-6-0PT 3616 steams past Tramway Junction box on 30 March 1965 with an inter-yard trip for Barnwood Sidings which has come from Quedgeley and called at Upper Yard. The wagons appear to be full of concrete sleepers manufactured at the Dow-Mac works, Quedgeley. The outward working to Quedgeley started from New Yard. In respect of inter-yard trips at Gloucester the working time table noted 'It should be understood by the whole of the staff concerned that these trips must be given special attention.'

John Goss

Above: Not just another picture of 0-6-0PT 3616 with another transfer on 29 March 1965, but a superb portrait of the railway; the loco with its exhaust piercing the sky; the two railwaymen ambling along the path; the variety of signals; Horton Road turntable; the Cathedral in the background – it could only be Gloucester! *John Goss*

Left, above: LMS 0-6-0T 1870 is in charge of shunting Upper Yard and Eastgate Goods Yard on 16 April 1946. This loco was withdrawn in April 1948 and never carried its BR number, 41870. The coal stage at the GWR shed is in the background, as is a 'Bulldog' 4-4-0. *E R Morten*

Left, below: 3F 0-6-0 43754 steams out of Upper Yard with what looks like a transfer trip to New Yard on 9 June 1962. Gloucester Goods Junction box is visible behind its train with Gloucester Passenger Station box on the right; both closed in March 1968. The tank behind the loco is the water softening plant. 43754 spent a lot of its LMS and the whole of its BR life allocated to Barnwood, being withdrawn in November 1962. Amongst its duties over the years the loco often worked the branch from Ashchurch to Upton-on-Severn including the last day of passenger trains on 12 August 1961. It also worked on the Nailsworth branch on the last day of regular passenger trains, 14 June 1947.

Above and right: Contrasting motive power on London trains, both heading towards Tramway. 5017 *St Donats Castle* departs for Paddington on 2 June 1952, while less exalted power, 0-6-0PT 9477, takes the train from London towards its ultimate destination, Cheltenham Spa St James, on 28 May 1960. Due to reversal by these trains at Central station, they were mainly worked by tank or smaller tender locos from Cheltenham to Gloucester, where a 4-6-0 – a 'Castle', 'Hall' or 'Modified Hall' took over. 9477 has a short train of just 5 coaches, but some of these workings consisted of 12 or 13 carriages, making the small locos bark a bit on the seven mile journey. Note the difference in the gantry and signals by the loco shed in these two views, the earlier having upper quadrants and the later with lower quadrants.   *E R Morten / B W L Brooksbank, Initial Photographics*

Right, below: 'Britannia' Pacific 70025 *Western Star* passes Horton Road shed in September 1959 with special working X02, probably from South Wales, as the loco was based at Cardiff Canton. When 'Britannias' were new in 1951, some class members were observed at Gloucester running in on Swindon line trains, and they worked Paddington expresses later in the 1950s. They were also sometimes seen in the harsh winter conditions of early 1963 filling in for failed diesels. Then near the end of steam in 1965, the class appeared regularly on summer Saturdays with holiday trains between Wolverhampton and Bristol via the Honeybourne line. *Author's collection*

Horton Road locomotive shed

Above: The loco shed has a good stock of typical engines on Sunday 3 August 1947, mostly Gloucester and Cheltenham based, but with a small number of visitors from Old Oak Common, Hereford, Worcester, South Wales and the West Midlands. The photographer recorded 61 locos on this visit. The shed on the right was originally meant for passenger locos, while the next two sheds were for goods locos. 0-6-0PT 4659 is close to the turntable, while the 2-6-2T on the same line appears to be 3175 of the 3150 class, often stationed at Brimscombe for banking duties.

B W L Brooksbank, Initial Photographics

Below: Shed pilot 0-6-0PT 2009 has ventured up the coal stage on 16 July 1949 with some fresh supplies to feed the locos below. Over the arch is a notice 'Caution – Engines must not pass this point.' A large water tank sits atop the lot. Gloucester still had a few of these old '1901' tanks at the time; 2009 was withdrawn in January 1951, while classmate 1996, which did not come to Gloucester until May 1951, lasted until January 1953.

W Potter, Kidderminster Railway Museum

Above: What a fine portrait of a rare locomotive type and staff at the old GWR Horton Road shed, perhaps posed for a special occasion. A 'Saint' class loco with the 4-4-2 'Atlantic' wheel arrangement, 172 *The Abbot* was built in February 1905 and was initially named *Quicksilver*, changing in March 1907. The GWR built a small number of 4-4-2s to enable comparison with some French Atlantics which it acquired. 172 was rebuilt into a 4-6-0 in April 1912.　　　*R Wales collection*

Below: GWR 4-4-0 1126, a former Midland & South Western Junction Railway loco, rebuilt at Swindon Works in November 1928, sits in the yard at Horton Road. Some MSWJ locos worked from Gloucester shed after they were absorbed into GWR stock on 1 July 1923. 1126 was recorded by the RCTS as being in use as a stationary boiler somewhere in Gloucester Docks in mid-1937. It returned to traffic afterwards and was the last MSWJ 4-4-0, withdrawn in December 1938.

B J Miller collection

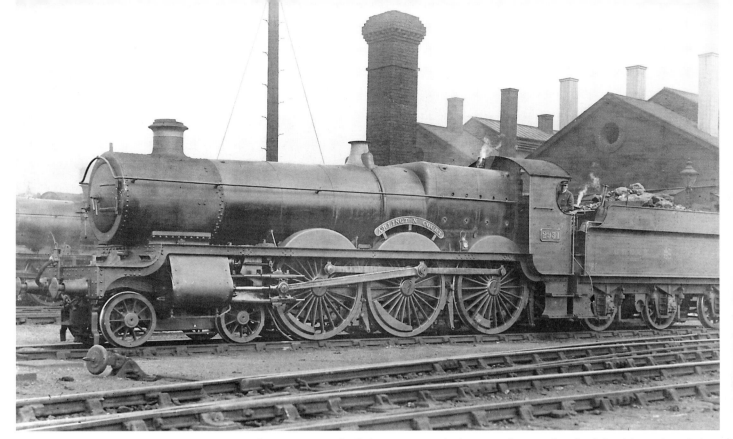

Above: Churchward 'Saint' 4-6-0 2931 *Arlington Court*, built in 1911, awaits its next duty at the shed, in this undated view sometime before it was fitted with outside steam pipes in 1937. The engine lasted into the BR era, being withdrawn in February 1951. Horton Road's last 'Saint' was 2951 *Tawstock Court*, withdrawn in June 1952. *Photomatic*

Below: In GWR days Horton Road had a small allocation of 'Aberdare' class 2-6-0s for freight work. 2680 is on shed on 9 April 1939, paired with an ex-ROD tender. It was one of a small number of the class which survived into BR days, at Hereford, but was withdrawn in 1948. Classmate 2656 lasted at Gloucester until March 1948. *RCTS*

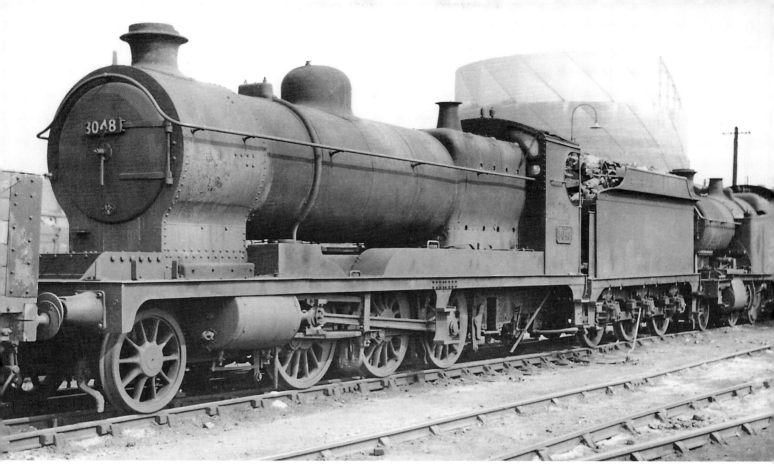

Above: ROD 2-8-0 3048 was allocated at Horton Road for many years, usually with one other of the class. One train originating at Gloucester and booked for 2-8-0 haulage was the 7.50pm class E Docks Branch Sidings to Llandilo, while the 6.13 pm class H Cheltenham High Street to Severn Tunnel Junction also had a 2-8-0. But 3048 is going nowhere on 24 August 1955, being under repair with its trailing driving wheels removed. Gloucester was never overblessed with an allocation of 2-8-0s considering how many there were on the Western Region, though plenty came on shed from other depots. Two Churchward 2-8-0s – 2809 and 2854 – transferred in to replace the RODs in the mid-1950s. There were also WD 2-8-0s on the roster – one was 90691, allocated here for most of the 1950s.

R K Blencowe collection

Right, above: Upon closure of Barnwood loco depot in May 1964, the remaining engines and crews transferred to the ex-GW shed. 4F 44264 with a Bristol Barrow Road shed plate blows off in Horton Road yard in this undated picture. It was actually allocated here from May 1965 until withdrawal in November, though it had also been a Barnwood loco in earlier times. Western crews did not always get on too well with these Midland designed engines!

Right, below: An Old Oak Common engine, 5035 *Coity Castle* occupies Horton Road's 65ft turntable on 14 June 1957. It has probably arrived in Gloucester on a Paddington-Cheltenham working. *R K Blencowe collection*

Tramway Junction to Midland station and Tuffley Junction

Left. above: A good 1964 view devoid of trains reveals various features including: the Passenger Station signal box; Eastgate yard behind it; the GW goods yard and goods shed on the right of the line into Central station. *Joe Moss collection, Roger Carpenter*

Left. below: In early LMS days, Midland 2P 4-4-0 466 blows off as it waits to leave the turntable located close to Eastgate yard, installed to save engines having to run out to turn at Barnwood shed. Behind the loco are the GWR carriage sidings and East Signal Box in the position it occupied until 1931. While these 4-4-0s were still frontline express power at the time, in BR days they mainly did pilot work on expresses, stopping services and station pilot duties. Another important turn for a 2P was the 5.53am fish train from Birmingham to Gloucester, arrive 7.56am, having stopped at Bromsgrove, Worcester, Ashchurch and Cheltenham. This was a light duty, just two or three vans, but important, and, of course, it did not run Mondays when fresh fish was not available. After its arrival, the whole station would naturally smell of fish. *B J Miller collection*

Below: It looks like the shape of things to come at the LMS station on 2 March 1938 – this Armstrong-Whitworth 3-car articulated diesel unit was on a test run from Derby. The unit ran public services, though not around Gloucester, until the outbreak of war in September 1939, but did not fare well afterwards, being cannibalised in 1949. *R G Jarvis, Midland Railway Trust*

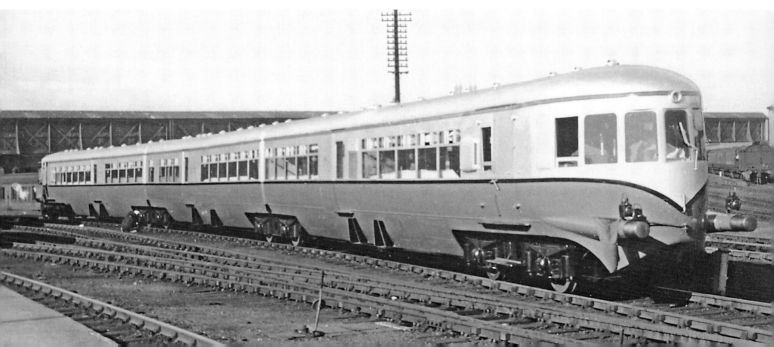

Compound 4-4-0 1024 of shed 8, Bristol, draws forward with its train on 18 March 1933, signalled into the head shunt, before reversing into the bay platform. It is the 6.45am slow from Bristol to Worcester and Birmingham, due in Gloucester at 8.25am, but not leaving until 8.57am. The train is vacating the platform to make way for the 7.52am Bristol – Bradford express. Gloucester Cathedral is glimpsed in the background.

E R Morten

Left, above: Barnwood based Fowler 2-6-2T 40040 is engaged on pilot duties in 1952. Larger Midland tank locos – 2-6-2T and 2-6-4T – did not have a great association with Gloucester, but 40040 was utilised to work Ashchurch-Great Malvern trains. It is fitted with condensing gear for use on commuter services through Moorgate and some other stations on the London Underground system, where this class was much more at home. After the Great Malvern branch was cut back to Upton-on-Severn at the end of November 1952, there was no real need for this loco and by January 1953 it was reallocated to join others of the class at Cricklewood shed, London. A Stanier 2-6-2T, 40116, also spent a while allocated to Barnwood, but normally sub-shedded at Tewkesbury, for Great Malvern trains.
R K Blencowe collection

Left, below: An unidentified 'County' 4-6-0 oozes steam as it gets away from Eastgate just after 5pm on the up 'Cornishman' from Penzance to Wolverhampton in the early 1950s. This Western Region train was notable for utilising the Midland route out of Bristol, via Mangotsfield, rather than the GW line via Stapleton Road, then joining the Midland at Yate. In 1952, the down 'Cornishman', which left Gloucester at 11.22am, still included a slip carriage for Taunton according to the public time table.

Below: A view dated 20 May 1973 of the ex-Midland Railway goods depot, located between Eastgate and Central stations. The shed had been on the same spot since at least the 1880s and, when built, was between the Midland Railway terminus station and the Midland main line.
RCTS

Above: Deeley 0-4-0T 41537 has some shunting to perform in Upper Yard, possibly as part of its Saturday duties when it returned from Gloucester Docks. In the right background are the wagon repair sheds. A Midland Railway lamp post and a water column complete with brazier provide additional interest to this scene which dates from the 1950s.

Author's collection

Below: 4F 44269 shunts in the sidings at Upper Yard, across from Eastgate station, in August 1965. Part of the loco's duties included a trip on the Hempsted branch. By this date, 4Fs, so familiar for years at Gloucester, were thin on the ground. 44269's fireman Dick Courtney, who took the picture, had classmate 44264 on the Hempsted duty the following week. Both locos were withdrawn later in the year.

R Courtney

Left, above: The long reign of Midland 2P and 4P Compound 4-4-0s drew to a close as more modern motive power became available to replace them, which came in the shape of BR Standard Class 4 4-6-0s. Barnwood received 75009 and 75023 in August 1958. Barrow Road's 75022 has an up local, the 9.15am from Bristol, on 13 April 1959.

B W L Brooksbank

Left, below: Summer Saturdays saw quite a lot of fairly rare locos appear, particularly from the North Western lines of the London Midland Region. This unrebuilt 'Patriot' 45541 *Duke of Sutherland* fits into that category, being from shed 2A Rugby. It is not on a holiday relief train, however, but the regular 8.40am Bristol to Newcastle on 23 July 1960. Three of the class, 45504, 45506 and 45519, were shedded at Bristol Barrow Road at the time, so were regularly seen at Gloucester. In the adjacent platform is a GW 2-6-2T with the 10.15am local to Worcester – this train had the task of stopping at Elm Bridge to set down water cans for the signal box.

Below: Despite the arrival of BR Standards, 2P 40501 was allocated to Barnwood for a few weeks in July and August 1960 before being withdrawn, but it did useful work as station pilot, while on 4 July it worked the 7.42am stopper to Bristol. This portrait, in superb evening light, shows it shunting a couple of horse boxes; a simple enough movement which nevertheless entailed working outside station limits and over Tramway Crossing. *John Goss*

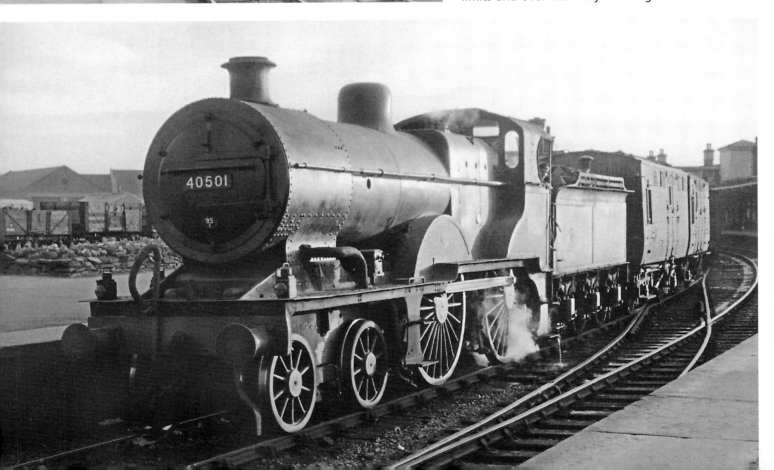

Right: Immaculate 4-2-2 'Spinner' 614 awaits departure on a down train in 1913, with a fine clerestory carriage behind the engine. The Johnson single wheelers were seen in the area into LMS days, often assisting express trains. Barnwood had some of the last of the type in service.   *R S Carpenter collection*

Below: A couple of 4-4-0s wait to move off in this view dated 7 April 1932; the loco in the platform is a class 3 with a stopping train. On the right a line of cattle wagons are parked on a siding.   *Mowat collection*

Right: The elevated Barton Street signal box has a commanding view of the scene, with B1 4-6-0 61313 in the station on 2 June 1962 heading relief train 1V40, the 7.40am Sunderland-Bristol. The author remembers one occasion when he saw two ex-LNER locos at Eastgate – a B1 and a K3 2-6-0. Thirty years on from the picture above, the lower quadrant signals have been replaced by upper quadrants. *S V Blencowe collection*

Above: Caprotti 'Black Five' 44753 arrives at Eastgate on 12 August 1961 with train 1N46, 8.40am Bournemouth-Bradford, which ran on Saturdays from 15 July to 26 August that year, one of the seemingly unceasing procession of northbound trains through Gloucester on those summer afternoons. 'Peak' diesels had commenced work on some services from June 1961, but the majority were still steam. This particular train will run non-stop from Gloucester to Birmingham New Street, except for pausing at Bromsgrove to get banking assistance up the Lickey Incline. *N E Preedy*

Left: Barton Street has changed rather a lot since this photo was taken on 17 January 1961 of 'Black Five' 44858 arriving on an up express. Plenty of warm overcoats are on display as well as some hats and a fine hairstyle! On the far right there is an advertising billboard for special excursion trains. Road traffic is very light, just a Gloucestershire Marketing Society lorry waits to cross. *Gordon Coltas*

Left, below: Gloucester had two city centre railway stations, one GWR and one LMS, but none in the suburbs. However it did have a tramway system for some years to transport citizens to and from the centre and this portrait shows Gloucester Corporation car 2 at Barton Street gates on the 'Tuffley & Cross' service in 1927. The tramcar was built by Brush Electrical Co in 1903. The fine LMS hoarding advertises some enticing excursion trips to Bath, Bournemouth and Weston-Super-Mare for those who could afford them. *R B Parr*

Above: With Barton Street box in the background, local engine 44045 makes a rousing and smoky exit along the down line towards Tuffley. It displays a tall chimney, curved top tender and 'LMS' initials, all of which had been replaced in its later years. The nearest line is the docks branch from High Orchard and the picture is close to the old Pembroke Street crossing, which came before California Crossing. Just visible beneath Barton Street signal box is a small ground frame cabin which was used until December 1960.

Below: California Crossing Signal Box was still in use when this picture was taken on 14 November 1975, albeit reduced to a ground frame from August 1968. There had been a box here since the late 1870s, but this particular one dates from September 1920. Happily it got preserved, first at the Dowty Railway Preservation site at Ashchurch, now at the North Gloucestershire narrow gauge railway at Toddington, where it still functions as a signal box. *M J Squire*

Left, above: The small crossing keeper's hut at Bowley's Crossing, Farm Street, is boarded up in this picture dated 23 January 1976. In earlier days, it was a signal box, though was not a block post. Though the lines between Eastgate and Tuffley are still in place, trains officially ceased running on this section from 1 December 1975. *S V Blencowe collection*

Left, below: Painswick Road Crossing signal box was opened on 15 October 1893 and was about three-quarters of a mile from Gloucester Midland station on the Stonehouse Junction line. By the date of this photo, 3 May 1969, it had been officially downgraded to a ground frame. The view is looking towards Tuffley Junction. Interestingly, three boxes in a row – California Crossing, Bowley's Crossing and this one – were all acquired for preservation. *M A King*

Below: Caprotti valve gear BR Standard 73142 heads out of Gloucester on a down express in August 1959. The engine was still relatively new, going into traffic in December 1956. There was a batch of ten of these Caprotti Standards on the LMR Midland Division, so they were frequent visitors to Gloucester at the time. *S Rickard collection, Brian Miller*

Local 4F 44035 vigorously attacks the 1 in 108 gradient of Tuffley bank with a coal train. Bankers could be requested on this section and there was often a west end pilot at Eastgate in the summer peak period ready to bank heavy holiday trains.

S Rickard, Brian Miller collection

High Orchard and Hempsted branches

Above: Midland Railway built 4F 43924, now preserved, steams along the double track section of the High Orchard branch by the park with a short freight from the docks. The date is 4 June 1962 and there was a note on the back of the print which said 'Back to Nature' referring to the overgrown track on the left. *W Potter*

Below: While four coupled tank locos prevailed at High Orchard, this 0-6-0ST also saw use. Built by Fox, Walker & Co of Bristol in 1878, works number 377, it was purchased secondhand by the Midland Railway in 1880. The date of this picture is not known. 2067A was broken up in 1906.

Right, above: Midland Railway 0-4-0ST 1142A, built in 1903, still looks pretty new in this picture of it shunting in Llanthony Road. The rerailing jack, lamps and rope also appear new. During 1904, the chimney had been shortened by four inches and a rear sheet was ordered for the cab. Also of note is that the train staff for the 'one engine in steam' branch is held outside the loco cab. A representative of this class lasted at Gloucester until 1932.

Right, below: In 1932 a new type of 0-4-0ST was built for the LMS by Kitsons of Leeds and 1540, the first of five in the class, is depicted at High Orchard on 5 June 1933. It was soon renumbered 7000. A further five of the class, incorporating detail alterations, were built by BR in 1953.

Below: Gloucester Railway Carriage & Wagon Co Ltd was connected to the Midland Railway in the docks and had its own shunting locos for many years up to 1961. The last was a Bagnall 0-4-0 fireless of 1947 named *Badgeworth Hall*. In July 1912 GRCW acquired an ex-GWR 0-4-0ST numbered 1391 and named *Fox*, seen at the works on 13 April 1933. The loco, built by Avonside Engine Co of Bristol in 1872, works number 913, retained its GWR number and name for the whole of its career at GRCW, being sent for scrap to Cashmores at Newport in March 1948. *Badgeworth Hall* went for scrapping to Hayes Metals on the GW side of the docks in March 1963.

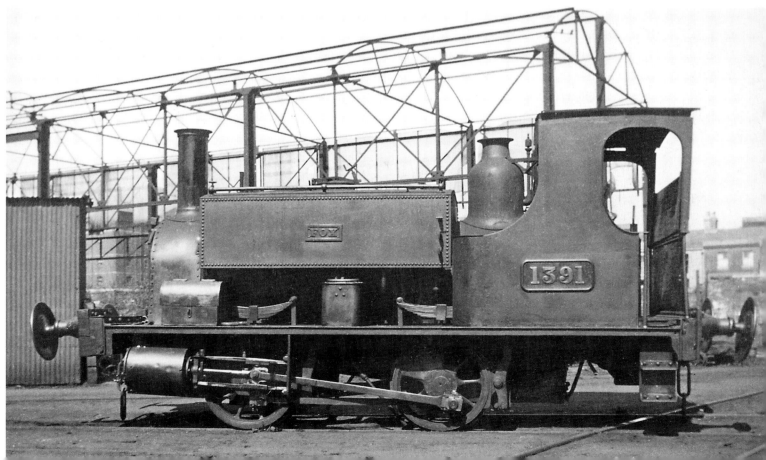

Above: Another type which appeared in the docks was the former Lancashire & Yorkshire Railway 'Pug' 0-4-0ST. It is 24 April 1948 at High Orchard, but 11212, with 'LMS' on its tank, has yet to adapt to the new BR order. This loco was normally shedded at Bristol, so was probably only on loan at Gloucester. After the 1923 Grouping, the LMS tried L&Y 0-6-0 tender locos for a while on the Stroud and Nailsworth branches; three were in store at Barnwood shed in 1935.

W Potter, Kidderminster Railway Museum

Left, above: With the above exception, Deeley 0-4-0Ts monopolised shunting in the docks during BR days until dieselisation in the 1960s. Indeed, 41530, withdrawn from Gloucester in 1957, had first worked at the docks when brand new in late 1907. These tanks were unusual for Midland Railway locos in having outside cylinders. 41537 was a regular performer and is seen in this feature filled portrait at High Orchard. It was reported to be in poor condition in 1951, but survived a visit to Derby Works, getting overhauled not scrapped. After another overhaul at Derby, in February 1961, it ran hot boxes on the return journey, needing attention at Barnwood before resuming work. It then worked on at Gloucester until withdrawal in September 1963.

Author's collection

Left, below: Deeley 0-4-0T 41535 chuffs alongside the Canal with a couple of wagons on 4 June 1962. 41535 left Gloucester for repair at Derby in April 1963 and then saw further service in Swansea docks, finally being withdrawn in autumn 1964.

W Potter, Kidderminster Railway Museum

Gloucester Gasworks was east of the Ship Canal and about one and a half miles from the city centre. According to the Industrial Railway Society it was connected to the Hempsted branch sometime after 1920. In August 1965, 4F 44269 is on the daily trip working, first seen at the gasworks with empty wagons. The second view shows it in the branch sidings; the gasworks connection goes off left by the engine, while the line to Hempsted Wharf curves to the left in the background. The line to Monk Meadow, which traversed a swing bridge across the canal, was straight ahead but this section had closed by May 1938. The third picture has 44269 bringing the empties towards Tuffley Junction.   *R Courtney*

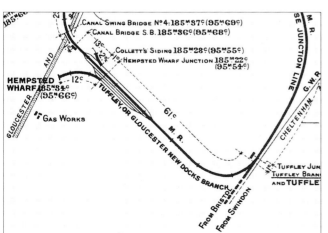

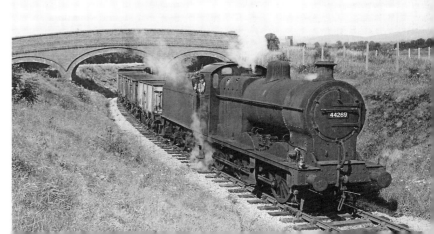

Tramway Junction to Great Western station and Over Junction

Left, above: The South Wales to Newcastle train steams away from the GWR station behind a Mogul on 18 March 1933. The train was scheduled to depart Gloucester at 11.2am. for its long cross-country journey via Andoversford, Chipping Norton, Banbury and the ex-Great Central route through the East Midlands. The LNER coaches will have worked down the previous day, while a GWR set would be coming in the opposite direction on this date. *E R Morten*

Left, below: A wartime evacuee is seen at Gloucester, in the shape of LNER 0-6-0 2072 on 9 April 1946. A number of these as well as some Southern Railway locos, including Class K10 4-4-0s, were drafted into the area during the war. It has to be said they were fairly ancient types and may have been viewed by the local footplatemen as more of a hindrance than a help, but they did their bit for the cause. They had all gone from the area before Nationalisation, as had the modern United States Army Transportation Corps 2-8-0s which also worked through Gloucester. *E R Morten*

Below: The 11.45am Cheltenham-London Paddington is photographed from Eastgate station on 13 April 1959 as it heads towards Central behind large Prairie tanks 5194 and 5198. It soon left this way, from the down platform, behind a – hopefully – gleaming 5094 *Tretower Castle*, which would have crossed to the up line by the time it passed the loco shed. *B W L Brooksbank*

Right, above and below: Two pictures at the up end of the GWR station. The goods shed is on the left, while the Gloucester East Signal Box seen in the first view was replaced in July 1931 by the one seen in the second picture, which also shows Large Prairie tank 5184 departing from the down platform with a Paddington-Cheltenham Spa train on 21 August 1963. In earlier times, the track going off to the right in both pictures connected with the lines into the old Midland Railway terminus station, which closed to passenger traffic in April 1896; the lines were retained as sidings.

Clinker Views, Brunel University Transport collection;
G Coltas

Below: Not the Bullet Train, but the GWR's attempt at streamlining when it was all the rage in the 1930s. 5005 *Manorbier Castle*, a regular on the 'Cheltenham Spa Express' or 'Cheltenham Flyer', is seen with the full streamlining in 1935 waiting to back onto the train for London. Compare the loco here with the picture of it on page 92 – some bits had been removed by 1936.

Left, above: GWR 2-4-0 588 of the '481' class stands in the up through road, believed to be in 1906. The class was built at Swindon in 1869 in anticipation of the standard gauging of various lines, including that through Gloucester to South Wales. 588 was rebuilt with a Belpaire boiler in 1915, before being withdrawn from service in 1919.

P J T Reed, V R Webster collection, Kidderminster Railway Museum

Left, below: The 'Buffalo' tanks did sterling work for many years, including hauling coal trains up from South Wales through Gloucester. This one, 1635, is absolutely immaculate after its conversion from saddle tank to pannier tank in 1911. It later spent time working fom Bullo Pill shed, in 1912/13.

Below: With the GWR goods shed in the background, 'Duke' class 4-4-0 3260 *Mount Edgcumbe* awaits departure from the up platform. The loco, constructed in 1895, retains an old narrow cab with outside springs and a small 2000 gallon tender. Built for service on the gradients of Devon and Cornwall, a number of 'Dukes' later transferred to Gloucester and Cheltenham to replace 2-4-0s. 3260 was a Gloucester engine when pictured here and was withdrawn in April 1938. It was not quite the end of the story however, as 3260's boiler was used in June 1938 on the new 'Dukedog' class 4-4-0 9019, and the initial allocation of the latter was – Gloucester! *R K Blencowe collection*

Above: 2-8-0T 5213 stands on the up road with a through freight in 1946. A lot of goods trains stopped at Central for water and crew change. Before the Severn Tunnel was constructed, huge numbers of freights from and to South Wales came through Gloucester. What a sight it must have been to see heavy trains of South Wales coal bound for London and hauled by two double-framed 0-6-0ST struggling away from here, the tanks working as far as Swindon. But the route has remained important for freight to this day. *E R Morten*

Right, above: Large Prairie tank 4141, a familiar sight for many years, is attached to a local passenger train in this undated picture. It worked out of Cheltenham Malvern Road shed from new in 1946 and has the letters CHEL stencilled on the cylinder cover. There is a glimpse of a Chalford auto in the adjacent bay platform.

Right, below: Auto tank 1424 sits quietly in the up bay platform, while the auto trailer receives a good old-fashioned wash and brush up. While the 14XXs were the obvious motive power for the Chalford autos, other classes also worked them, such as the 5400 class 0-6-0T of which 5417 and 5418 were around for some time in 1950s. Non-availability of an auto-fitted loco meant Prairie tanks sometimes appeared on the workings as did various non-auto fitted 0-6-0PT. There was even a memorable occasion when a Collett 2-8-0 was turned out, probably as a last resort, to haul the one-coach train! *R Stanton*

Above: A new 4-6-0, 7815 *Fritwell Manor*, was shedded at Gloucester in 1939 to work the Swansea to Newcastle train but it is classmate 7810 *Draycott Manor* which is seen at the station with the train on 21 June 1939, with GWR coaches. The service was cancelled upon the outbreak of war a couple of months later and took a different route when it resumed in the post-war period. 7810 was allocated to Gloucester for several years in the mid-1950s and 7815, after working at various sheds in BR days, was back at Gloucester when withdrawn in 1964.

V R Webster, Kidderminster Railway Museum

Left, above: At the down platform 'Star' class 4-6-0 4036 *Queen Elizabeth*, shedded at Swindon, has backed onto a local train, probably from Cheltenham, brought in by a small Prairie tank in the late 1940s. Headboards on the carriages indicate these will be worked through to Paddington after being attached to another train at Swindon.

W Dendy

Left, below: Small Prairie tank 4564 made a welcome reappearance in the area towards the end of steam. It had been a local engine for at least the whole BR period until transferred elsewhere in 1958. Then it came back and resumed duties on Cheltenham to Gloucester trains as if it had never been away. The loco puffs past the down platform on 25 October 1963 after being released from a Cheltenham train, which has departed towards Swindon. The milk machine on the platform brings back to the author the taste of strawberry flavoured milk shakes purchased from it in trainspotting days.

B W L Brooksbank

Three trains at the platforms at Central in the mid-1950s. 4358 has come in from the Grange Court direction, the train is the 2.25pm from Hereford, due at 3.40pm. A large Prairie tank awaits departure at the down platform while the diesel railcar is on the 3.20pm from Cheltenham, going forward as the 4.8pm to Ledbury. Having two trains together on the down side allowed the 3.0pm from Chalford to arrive further along the platform at 3.42pm.   *P J Shoesmith*

ROYAL TRAIN GLOSTER G.W.R JUNE 23 09

Above: King Edward VII visited the Royal Agricultural Society of England Show at Gloucester on 23 June 1909 and here is the Royal Train in the station at the down platform behind brand new 'Star' class 4-6-0 4021 named, of course, *King Edward*, carrying the standard GWR Royal Train headlamps and side shield. The train was due to arrive at midday to be greeted by various dignitaries and leave at 4.30pm. When Queen Victoria changed trains at Gloucester on 29 September 1849, Her Majesty, like ordinary passengers, was forced to experience the inconvenience of the break of gauge, arriving from Derby on a standard gauge Midland Railway train and leaving by the broad gauge GWR. This view shows the prominence of Middle Signal Box sitting on top of the footbridge. Apart from closure and removal of the box, the station did not alter much for the next sixty years or so, until the substantial changes wrought in 1968.

Left, above: Mogul 7318 drifts down into Central with a short freight, possibly from Hereford, on 29 June 1964. There were three scheduled freights from Hereford to Gloucester, the lunchtime arrival terminated at Old Yard, while the two late evening arrivals went to New Yard. West Signal Box in the background controlled movements at this end of the station.

Left, below: A number of 'Bulldog' class 4-4-0s survived in the area after Nationalisation. The Gloucester to Hereford service was a favourite duty for them and 3406 *Calcutta* in this picture has a newly applied 85C Hereford shedplate. The *Railway Observer* noted, 'As 1951 dawned 3406 *Calcutta*, rusty and exuding steam from many parts, was still hard at work from Hereford on the passenger turns to Gloucester. This is probably the last 'Bulldog' on daily passenger work.' Sadly, 3406 was withdrawn later in January and the whole class had gone well before the end of 1951. *Author's collection*

Above: Following the damage to and closure of the Severn Bridge in October 1960, schoolchildren who used to travel four miles over the bridge between Lydney and Sharpness found themselves being transported the long way round, a trip of nearer forty miles. 0-6-0PT 6437 has the duty on 5 June 1962; it had a booked water stop at Central on the up through line, so there was no getting off. The unadvertised train left Lydney Junction at 3.30pm, due Sharpness at 4.37pm; via the Severn Bridge, the journey had taken 12 minutes. Gloucester West signal box is on the right. *Alan Jarvis*

Below: The broad gauge through Gloucester was removed in 1872. On Saturday 11 May the 12.40 pm from Gloucester to New Milford, in West Wales, ran on the broad gauge for the last time; just twelve hours later, the 12.50am night mail ran out of Gloucester for South Wales on the narrow (standard) gauge. The up line from Gloucester to Swindon was narrow gauged and ready for trains on Sunday 26 May, while the down line was completed on the following Wednesday. Broad Gauge 4-4-0ST *Hesiod* is pictured between the station and London Road bridge around 1870. Coupled to it is a wagon used for transporting horse-drawn carriages, a throwback to the earliest days of passenger carrying railways.

Bleasdale, Kidderminster Railway Museum

Gloucester Docks Branch

Above: A good view of Over Junction with spark arrester fitted dock shunter 1616 moving off the Ledbury branch onto the main line. The daily freight to Ledbury started from Docks Branch Sidings, which curves off to the right. The main line to Gloucester goes under the bridge. 1616's spark arrester was deemed necessary for locos required to shunt petrol tank wagons in the docks. Other class members shedded at Horton Road so fitted at various times included 1605 and 1623. One loco was diagrammed to shunt Docks Branch Sidings and Over Sidings while another worked between Docks Branch Sidings and the docks.

Left, above: Mixed traffic 4-6-0 4956 *Plowden Hall* has charge of an up parcels train from South Wales at Over Junction on 13 April 1962, as a 2-8-0 stands in the up loop with a minerals working. On the left is the junction to the Great Western's Gloucester Docks Branch Sidings, while, on the right, just in front of the signal box, is the branch that formerly went to Ledbury, truncated by this date to terminate at Dymock.

B W L Brooksbank, Initial Photographics

Left, below: Getting this northbound train out of Docks Branch Sidings on 5 May 1959 involves the interesting manoeuvre of propelling it onto the South Wales main line. While 0-6-2T 6690 does its work at the other end, the guard is 'keeping a sharp look-out'. This was all in accordance with rules and regulations which further stated that: 'Trains must not be propelled from the Docks Branch Sidings to the Up Main Line at Over Junction – trains for the direction of Gloucester must be propelled to the Down Loop or Down Main and afterwards pass to the Up Main through the crossover at Over Junction.'

M Hale

Left: An interesting use for the line from Docks Branch Sidings to Over Junction in the 1950s was the transfer of heavy, out-of-gauge loads between road and rail and back to road. In the early post-war years, the Central Electricity Generating Board was constructing new generating stations at Uskmouth, Newport and Aberthaw, which needed huge transformers and stators, weighing up to 145 tons. While being too big to do the whole journey from the manufacturers by rail, they were also too heavy for the road bridges across the River Severn. The solution was to make handling points at Docks Branch Sidings and Over Junction and shift these monsters very slowly and carefully on a 'Flatrol' EAA special wagon. The picture shows one such load being manoeuvred past a signal gantry; anything which fouled the load had to be removed and then replaced.

Below: Docks Branch Sidings hosts a stranger on a snowy 14 January 1963 with a 4-wheeled Sentinel diesel undertaking some shunting trials, while more traditional power in the shape of 0-6-0PT 8701 stands alongside. By this date shunting on the branch and in the docks on the Western side was already diagrammed for the standard BR 204hp 0-6-0 shunters in the D2000 series. A Brush Bagnall diesel shunter was also tried in the Midland side of the docks, which was still the preserve of the Deeley 0-4-0T at the time.

B J Ashworth

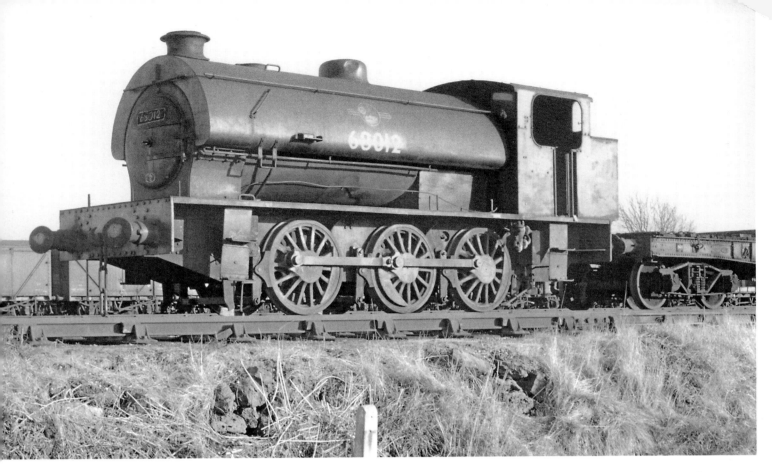

Above: J94 0-6-0ST 68012 stands in Docks Branch Sidings, the last of its class on BR, withdrawn in October 1967. It was one of 75 of this type purchased from the Ministry of Supply by the LNER after the war. 68012 never worked in the area, but had been towed down from Westhouses in Derbyshire and was on its way to a scrapyard in Newport. Many identical locos, originally built for the War Department, were still in industrial service in the late 1960s, particularly with the National Coal Board. In March 1963, J94 68070, sold out of service by BR, was at Barnwood shed *en route* to South Wales for further use in the coal industry. Others seen in the area included WD125 and WD179, hauled dead through Gloucester in the 6.40am Hinksey to Roger-stone freight on 23 January 1961 being transferred from the Army base at Bicester to the NCB's Tredegar workshops. *Author's collection*

Left: Except for the class 03 diesel shunter, the view above at Llanthony in 1967 still portrays the steam era. The picture below shows the yard in December 1981. On the left is the ex-GWR goods shed and offices. Part of the Blue Circle Cement complex can be seen on the right. Further to the right were lines to Monkmeadow where there were more sidings, including those of Hayes Metal Ltd who cut up a few ex-GWR steam locos in the 1960s.

W Potter, Kidderminster Railway Museum;
S V Blencowe collection

Above, left: The *Great Western Railway Magazine* recorded an unfortunate accident at the docks on 2 March 1909 when a steam crane being used to lift a boiler broke away from its moorings and fell into the canal together with its load. The picture shows parts of the crane loaded onto trucks. The salvage operation was assisted by divers from the docks company.

Above, Right: This unusual signal in the docks was spotted and photographed on 19 July 1959. The single story building in the background bears the legend 'Gloucester Shipyard Ltd'.   *P J Garland, R S Carpenter collection*

Below: Gloucester Corporation Electricity Department opened a small coal fired power station, Castle Meads, on the banks of the River Severn in 1941, with railway connections to Docks Branch Sidings. In 1942 a fireless 0-4-0 arrived from Andrew Barclay & Co of Kilmarnock to do the internal shunting. The plant was nationalised in 1948, eventually becoming part of the Central Electricity Generating Board. The loco worked until 1969, but was retained in good condition, being presented to the Dowty Railway Preservation Society at Ashchurch in late 1974. It is now appropriately preserved at Gloucester Docks, whose warehouses are in the background of the picture.   *M J Squire*

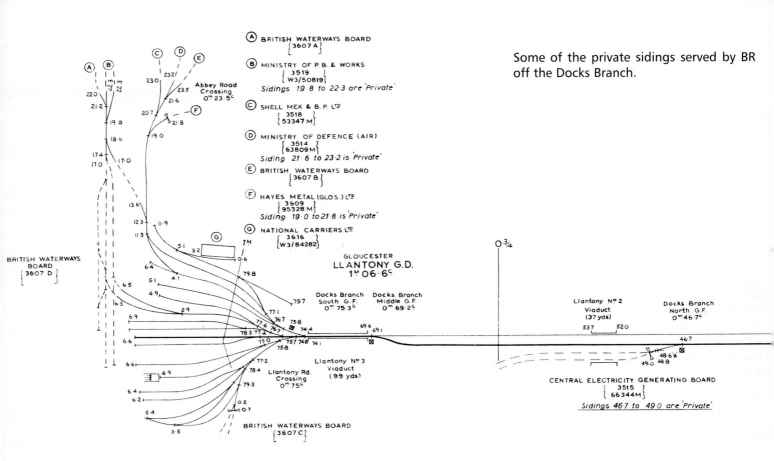

Some of the private sidings served by BR off the Docks Branch.

(A) BRITISH WATERWAYS BOARD
{ 3607 A }

(B) MINISTRY OF P.B. & WORKS
{ 3519 }
{ W3/50819 }
Sidings 19·8 to 22·3 are 'Private'

(C) SHELL MEX & B.P. LTD
{ 3518 }
{ 53347 M }

(D) MINISTRY OF DEFENCE (AIR)
{ 3514 }
{ 63809M }
Siding 21·6 to 23·2 is 'Private'

(E) BRITISH WATERWAYS BOARD
{ 3607 B }

(F) HAYES METAL (GLOS.) LTD
{ 3609 }
{ 95328 M }
Siding 19·0 to 21·8 is 'Private'

(G) NATIONAL CARRIERS LTD
{ 3616 }
{ W3/84282 }

GLOUCESTER
LLANTONY G.D.
1ᴹ 06·6ᶜ

Abbey Road Crossing 0ᵐ 23·5ᶜ

BRITISH WATERWAYS BOARD
{ 3607 D }

Docks Branch South G.F. 0ᵐ 75·3ᶜ

Docks Branch Middle G.F. 0ᵐ 69·2ᶜ

Llantony Rd. Crossing 0ᵐ 75ᶜ

Llantony Nº 3 Viaduct (99 yds)

BRITISH WATERWAYS BOARD
{ 3607 C }

O ¾

Llantony Nº 2 Viaduct (37 yds)

Docks Branch North G.F. 0ᵐ 46·7ᶜ

CENTRAL ELECTRICITY GENERATING BOARD
{ 3515 }
{ 66344M }
Sidings 46·7 to 49·0 are 'Private'

South Wales main line to Lydney

Left: At Over was the junction for the Ledbury branch. Dymock station, about twelve miles along the line, presents a lovely picture looking towards Gloucester with a GW diesel railcar and – passengers! The yard looks busy too and the local pick-up freight from Gloucester continued until withdrawal in June 1964. Although always a single line from Over Junction, the earthworks allowed for a double track, which it had been from here to Ledbury until 1917. What a shame the passenger train service from Gloucester was withdrawn on and from 13 July 1959, with the line being closed completely between Dymock and Ledbury from that date.

Roger Carpenter

Above: Oakle Street station, just over five miles from Gloucester Central, had a reasonable service, served mainly by Hereford and Cinderford trains. It was able to handle livestock including horse boxes and had a one and a half ton crane. This undated portrait is looking towards Grange Court.

Lens of Sutton

Below: Gloucester's ROD 2-8-0 3048 presents an impressive spectacle as it approaches Grange Court station on a down freight in the mid-1950s. On a class F express freight.

N E Preedy collection

Above: Grange Court station was well supplied with platforms, being the junction between the South Wales and Hereford lines. The view looking east was taken on 29 July 1932. The road approach to the station and the main buildings are on the right, down, side.

Mowat collection

Below: 7814 *Fringford Manor* starts the 10.28am ex Hereford on 17 August 1964, which has extra vehicles tacked on the end of the usual three carriages. The signal box in this picture replaced two earlier ones – West and East – in April 1935.

R K Blencowe

Above: Grange Court West box had been in the fork of the South Wales and Hereford lines but was gone by the time of this picture at the junction as Mogul 6380 arrives from Hereford while 2-8-2T 7247 waits in the main line loop. This was the scene of great activity back in August 1869 when the Hereford line was converted from broad to standard gauge. The method of doing this and the experience gained by the GWR was put to good use when the South Wales line and other routes on the system was converted from 1872.

R K Blencowe

Below: A quick look at the Hereford line emphasises its rural character, with Mogul 7301 at Longhope heading a train from Gloucester on 1 June 1952. At this time, there were eight passenger trains each way on weekdays, but no Sunday service. The usual motive power on the passengers were Moguls, with 'Manors' and 2-6-2T also performing. In the 1960s the 7.58am train from Swindon to Hereford often had a BR Standard class 4 2-6-4T. Workings such as pigeon specials brought bigger engines, with a 'Britannia' noted on at least one occasion.

E R Morten

Two interesting views at the west end of Newnham station in the early 1900s. 4-4-0 3546 pauses on a Gloucester to Newport local service with an assortment of carriages. 3546 had a quite remarkable existence – it had been built in the late 1880s as a broad gauge convertible 0-4-2ST, then rebuilt as an 0-4-4T, before being altered to standard gauge. It was rebuilt again, from 0-4-4T to 4-4-0 tender engine! In 1921 3546 went from the GWR to the Cambrian Railway to replace one of the locos destroyed in the Abermule disaster. In 1922 it was absorbed back into GWR stock, finally being withdrawn in 1927.

In the first picture, the Forest of Dean branch bay, where a 2021 class 0-6-0ST waits with a train to Cinderford, had not yet been built. Note also the difference in signals compared with the earlier view. While the branch, built partly on the former Bullo Pill tram road, had broad gauge goods trains from July 1854, converted to standard gauge from May 1872, it had to wait until April 1908 before the GWR introduced a passenger service between Newnham and the Severn & Wye station at Cinderford. Auto trailer working was authorised in 1910.　　　　　　　　　　　　　　　　　　　　　　　*Lens of Sutton*

Above: There was a nasty pile-up between Newnham and Bullo Pill in broad gauge days. The signalling system in use allowed for one train to follow another at a ten-minute interval, but this rule was far from foolproof. It was found wanting on 5 November 1868 when the up Milford mail ploughed into the back of a cattle train which had stopped with engine trouble. Six of the eight men in the cattle train's brake van were killed and 36 head of cattle also perished. No-one on the mail was killed or even injured, perhaps a testament to the sturdy construction of the broad gauge carriages. This early photograph shows the mail engine, 4-4-0 *Rob Roy*, one of the 'Waverley' class brought into service in 1855 for the South Wales main line as was in the years before the Severn Tunnel was built.

Below: This picture gives a good view of the Bullo Pill layout as a pannier tank crosses onto the steeply graded Forest of Dean branch in 1958 with a Cinderford passenger train. Just visible on the curve is the sand drag meant to slow any runaways down the 1 in 48 gradient. The signal box seen in this view is Bullo Pill West. There were a number of halts on the branch, with Bullo Cross being the closest, after which the train will go through Haie Hill tunnel, at 1064 yards the longest of three on the line. When the author travelled on the footplate of 0-6-0PT 3675 with the branch goods on 11 December 1965, he was advised to put a handkerchief over his mouth and nose through Hale Hill tunnel and to avoid breathing in the smoke, so the lads with their heads out of the window should get them back inside pretty soon! The passenger service was withdrawn on and from 3 November 1958, but goods trains continued; the branch closed in August 1967.   *E T Gill, R K Blencowe collection*

Left, above: There was a small engine shed at Bullo Pill dating from the broad gauge days of the 1850s; the picture shows the width of the building. It had a small allocation of goods locos, but closed in 1931 with locos and crews transferred to the ex-Severn & Wye shed at Lydney. *Rail Archive Stephenson*

Left, below: Awre & Blakeney station is depicted on 19 April 1958, with a view looking west. On the right the Forest of Dean Central Railway branch curves away towards Blakeney. It was used only for wagon storage by this date and the track had been lifted beyond Blakeney. On the main South Wales line to the left can be seen the abutments of a bridge which was to carry the branch to the River Severn. *H D Bowtell*

Below: Not an everyday sight near Awre is 'Dukedog' 4-4-0 9008 of 84E Tyseley shed. It is in charge of a down class 'H' freight on 9 August 1951. While the class is perhaps most associated with North Wales, there were a few at other sheds, such as Tyseley and Swindon. The circumstance in which 9008 came to be on the South Wales line from Gloucester is not known. *B W L Brooksbank, Initial Photographics*

Above: Ex-works 0-6-0PT 9609 skirts the Severn estuary as it approaches Lydney on quite a long down freight on 23 August 1963. This was a Llanelly engine so is presumably working its way home after attention at Swindon Works.

Alan Lewis Chambers

Below: This fine landscape shot taken on 27 August 1963 shows not only the glorious scenery of the area but also how the Severn Bridge enhances its surroundings. What a shame an accident ruined its useful existence. An iron ore train hauled by 9F 2-10-0 92228 has just passed under the stone arches carrying the Severn Bridge railway over the Gloucester to South Wales main line.

Alan Lewis Chambers

Above: A magnificent portrait on the Gloucester to South Wales line at Lydney Junction with 2-8-2T 7200 drifting through on a down freight. Various baskets, boxes and packages await dispatch on the platform.

R E Toop

Lydney to Standish Junction

Left, above: The former Severn & Wye Railway loco depot at Lydney Junction had quite a sizeable allocation in GWR days – amounting to 20 engines in 1947, though it had become a sub-shed of Gloucester in 1935. This view, dated 25 September 1962, includes 0-6-0PT 3775 and 1623; the 1600 class was particularly associated with Lydney and gradually took over from the old GWR tanks which had worked in the Forest of Dean for many years. By October 1951, 85B's allocation included eight 1600s and six of the older GWR 0-6-0PT with most being at Lydney. The depot closed on 29 February 1964. *R S Carpenter collection*

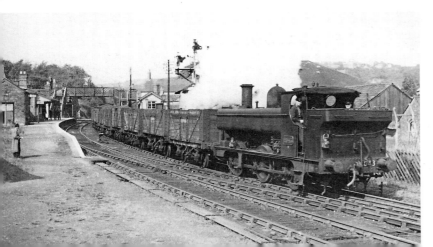

Left, below: Shifting coal was the main reason for the existence of the many tram roads and railways in the Forest of Dean and this delightful portrait shows ancient GWR 0-6-0PT 2043, with open back cab and storm sheet rolled up, bowling past Lydney Town with another load on 9 August 1947. *W A Camwell*

An excellent set of pictures, here and overleaf, taken on 3 June 1957 give a flavour of the Berkeley Road to Lydney route. The two coach auto train with 0-4-2T 1430 waits to draw forward into the platform as a down express with a Caprotti 'Black Five' approaches the station. The swing bridge over the Gloucester and Sharpness Canal is seen from 1430's footplate as it heads the train towards the Severn Bridge on its way to Lydney. As is well recorded, the Severn Bridge between Lydney and Sharpness suffered a fatal blow – literally – when it was hit and irreparably damaged on 27 October 1960. Before that, it proved useful as a diversionary route when the Severn Tunnel was closed for maintenance. The biggest locos allowed over it in latter days were 2-6-0s and these worked the regular Sunday diverted Bristol-South Wales trains and a daily Severn Tunnel Junction-Bristol freight.

Alan Jarvis

Having arrived at Lydney Town 1430 is propelling back before pulling forward into the opposite platform where a goodly number of passengers wait for the return trip. Finally the auto train is seen propelling away from Severn Bridge station heading back to Sharpness and Berkeley Road. Travelling from Berkeley Road to Lydney Junction and on to Gloucester provided an alternative to the direct route but presumably the fare was greater. The Severn & Wye Railway was allowed to charge extra mileage for passengers crossing the bridge.
Alan Jarvis

Above: A fine view at Sharpness Docks on 1 November 1952 from the high level BR connection with the swing bridge on the low level line, steam power on the water and a number of railway wagons ready for use.
Millbrook House Ltd

Right, above: There was a scrap yard in Sharpness Docks which received various withdrawn ex-BR steam locos for cutting up in the 1960s. Locos, including a 47XX 2-8-0, once the pride of the GWR and Swindon Works, await their grisly fate. *R Stanton*

Right, below: 4F 44123 draws a very short train away from Sharpness Docks on 11 April 1964 towards Docks Branch Junction (South).The mineral wagons to the left of the train are parked on the British Waterways Board lines, which were worked by its own diesels, of which there were two. There had been steam shunters in the docks, but the last was scrapped around May 1964. On the right of the picture are two sets of tracks; the main line between Berkeley and Sharpness is in the centre, with the goods lines to the right of them. There was a further connection into the docks north of Sharpness station. *W Potter, Kidderminster Railway Museum*

Leeds Holbeck based 'Jubilee' 45562 *Alberta* has charge of the 9.20am Bradford to Paignton on 7 July 1962 at Coaley Junction. This was a summer Saturday train and a relief to the 'Devonian', the latter normally being diesel hauled by this date.

Michael Mensing

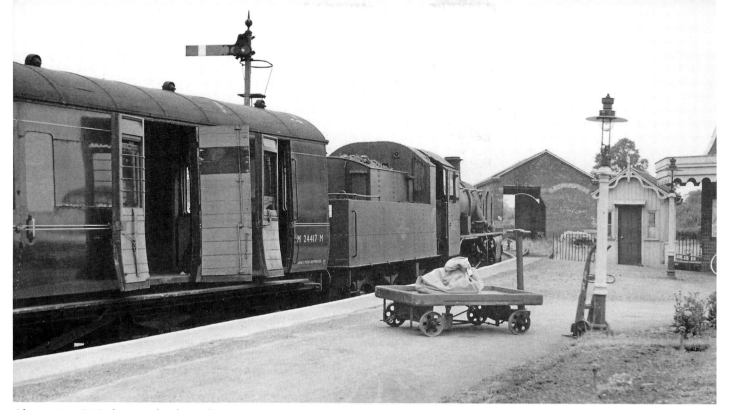

Above: In 1962 the Dursley branch was regularly worked by Ivatt Moguls 46526 and 46527; it is the latter seen on 7 July 1962 with the 7.40pm from Coaley. The picture has an interesting display of railway furniture and structures which all helped to create that wonderful atmosphere of the steam age. *Michael Mensing*

Below: 1600 class 0-6-0PT were the regular Dursley branch engines from the mid-1950s and one is at Dursley in this undated view. The branch had mixed trains until it ceased carrying passengers in September 1962 – the working time table showed the first train from Coaley, at 7am, and the last train from Dursley, at 7.5pm, were mixed. The schedule over the two and a half miles was the same – 9 minutes including a stop at Cam – whether trains were passenger or mixed. Motor trains were authorised between Gloucester and Coaley Junction, but not apparently on the branch. *E T Gill, R K Blencowe collection*

Tall chimneyed 4F 44203 heads a Westerleigh to Birmingham freight through the small wayside station at Frocester on 17 August 1960. The goods yard is very restricted and includes a small wagon turntable and a delightful stone goods shed. From 1918 to 1924 there had been a branch here to ballast pits. The station closed to passenger and goods on and from 17 December 1961.

H B Priestley, Milepost 92½; David Ibbotson

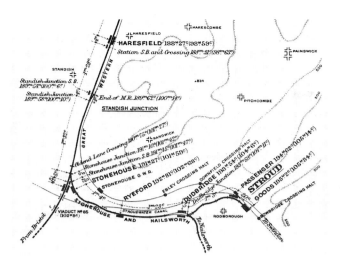

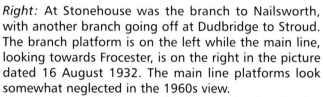

Right: At Stonehouse was the branch to Nailsworth, with another branch going off at Dudbridge to Stroud. The branch platform is on the left while the main line, looking towards Frocester, is on the right in the picture dated 16 August 1932. The main line platforms look somewhat neglected in the 1960s view.

Mowat collection; Author's collection

Below: It is 18 August 1932 at the modest and tranquil Stroud LMS station. There is an 0-4-4T beyond the platform with its single coach train, while a clerestory roofed carriage sits in the bay. Beyond the loco is the goods shed. *Mowat collection*

Freight services to Stroud and Nailsworth continued long enough to see diesel haulage, but steam was in charge when these pictures were taken on 21 and 23 July 1965 by Fireman Dave Smith. On the first date, 78004 shunts at Stroud Wallbridge while the guard and shunter stand by. Just visible in the centre of the picture is a signal on the GW line into Stroud. The other two pictures were taken on 23 July at Dudbridge Junction after the train had returned from Stroud with 78001 and show the fly shunting operation. The loco has left the wagons on the branch and run forward onto the Nailsworth line; the brakes on the van are released by the guard and the train drifts gently into Dudbridge before being halted. Further shunting takes place to park the wagons and get the brake van positioned to go behind the engine to Nailsworth. The wagons from Stroud will be collected on the return. Dudbridge Junction signal box was in the vee between the two lines; it closed in December 1957.

D L Smith

Above: The last LMS passenger time table before Nationalisation, for services from 6 October 1947, proclaims 'Service Suspended' for table 268 Nailsworth, Stroud and Stonehouse. The service had been 'temporarily' withdrawn from 16 June 1947, but was never reintroduced and the status was made permanent on and from 8 June 1949. However there were occasional excursion trains and rail tours after that date. 0-4-4 'Motor Tank' 1303 stands at Woodchester station on the Nailsworth branch in August 1940 with its single coach train. In 1938 there were eight advertised Monday – Friday departures from Nailsworth, with two more on Saturdays. Some worked through to Stonehouse and others went only to Dudbridge for connection into the Stroud to Stonehouse service. While most were 'Motors' a couple were ordinary passenger trains and the first departure from Nailsworth was a mixed.   *Lens of Sutton collection*

Below: 3F 3754 shunts at Nailsworth goods yard in June 1947. It was on a different level to the passenger station which had been located in anticipation of being on a through line to Malmesbury – but this never materialised, so Nailsworth remained at the end of a quiet branch.   *Millbrook House Ltd*

Standish Junction to Sapperton

Left, above: A Collett 2-8-0 shifts its class 'E' express freight away from Standish Junction on the Sapperton line. In the foreground is the Midland line to Bristol. In the earliest years of railways here, both lines had been broad gauge, but the Bristol & Gloucester was converted to mixed gauge in 1854 by the Midland Railway. It was 1872 before the Sapperton route was converted to standard gauge. *Author's collection*

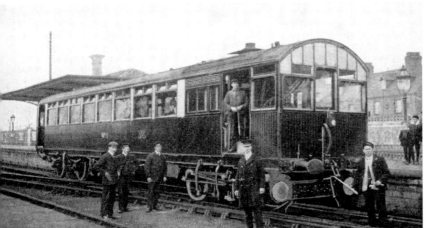

Left, below: Stonehouse to Chalford was the first service on the GWR to have steam rail motors, introduced in October 1903. The motors were seen as an economical way of running new local services including stops at places which were too small to have a full station. Initially some, like Downfield Crossing, did not have a platform, with passengers using adjustable steps on the rail motor to get on and off, though small halts were soon built. This posed picture of Steam Rail Motor No. 1 is at Stonehouse station, probably not long after the service, which quickly became very popular, was introduced. No.1 and its companion, No.2, were originally stabled at Chalford.

Below: 0-6-0PT 6412 (now preserved) stands at Stonehouse with the Chalford auto. This loco was at Gloucester for just a short time, from August 1964, and was withdrawn after the Chalford service ceased on 31 October 1964. There were others from this push-and-pull fitted class – and the similar 5400s – at Gloucester over the years, whose duties included the Chalford trains. *E T Gill, R K Blencowe collection*

Above: Passenger growth along the Stroud Valley meant the steam rail motors often needed to haul a trailer for which they were not best suited, so the GWR introduced auto, or motor, trains. The Collett 4800 (later 1400) class 0-4-2T came into service in 1932 for these duties and became indelibly associated with the Chalford autos. 1472 crosses the 132-yards long Watts Viaduct on the approach to Stroud station with a Chalford working. On the left behind the train is a siding which had a turntable at the end for getting wagons into the Stratford Mills of H Townsend & Co Ltd, whose siding was at right-angles to the main line.

Below: The Chalford service, pictured at Stroud on 17 March 1933, is headed by 'Metro' 2-4-0T 1459, fitted for auto train working. Gloucester had three 'Metro' tanks around this time – 1415, 1459 and 3561, so the new Collett 0-4-2T had not yet completely taken over. '2021' class 0-6-0ST and '517' class 0-4-2T were also used on Chalford trains in earlier years.

E R Morten

Above: Castle class 7000 *Viscount Portal*, a Gloucester Horton Road engine from June 1959 until February 1963, approaches Stroud with a down Cheltenham express. The solid Cotswold stone goods shed still exists complete with lettering, but not in railway use. Sadly the fine signal box has been demolished.   *A W V Mace collection, Milepost 92½*

Below: Collett 2-8-0 3858 has full steam on at Brimscombe with a down freight. The Thames & Severn canal which is in the foreground was sold to the GWR in 1881, who only wanted it to stop anyone else buying it. The GWR did not maintain the canal, so it became pretty well unnavigable.   *Gerald T Robinson*

Above: A study of Brimscombe station on 12 June 1962, looking towards Swindon.   *P J Garland, R S Carpenter collection*

Below: The Brimscombe banker, 2-6-2T 3173, is at the small shed on 2 June 1935. From Brimscombe the line climbed all the way to Sapperton, where the summit was between the two tunnels, with the steepest ascent being at 1 in 58. The shed and its banking engines had been located here since 1845, soon after the opening of the line, and the building's broad gauge origins can be seen in this portrait. With the onset of dieselisation the need for banking locos was reduced and the shed closed in early March 1965; bankers were thereafter provided from Gloucester Horton Road shed when required.

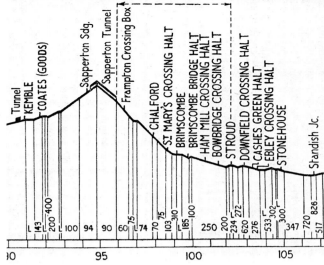

Left, above: The down 'Cheltenham Spa Express' passes St Mary's Crossing Halt on 12 June 1962 behind an unidentified 'Castle'. It left London Paddington at 5pm and arrived at Gloucester Central at 7.18pm, stopping only at Kemble and Stroud.

P J Garland, R S Carpenter collection

Left, below: The delightful scenery of the Golden Valley is shown to good effect in this picture of 7030 *Cranbrook Castle* with the 10.45am Paddington-Cheltenham express at St Mary's Crossing Halt between Chalford and Brimscombe on 3 October 1953. The loco is just passing over the Thames & Severn canal.

George Heiron, The Transport Treasury

Below: Mogul 6384 heads the 8.15am Margam to Moreton Cutting class 'E' freight on 23 March 1963, with a banker in the form of a 2-6-2T. The scene is near St Mary's Crossing which is in the background.

Gerald T Robinson

Right, above: An early view of Chalford shows part of the busy looking station and yard, including cattle pens, with a four coach train in the up platform and a 70ft auto trailer in a siding. *Photochrom / R K Blencowe collection*

Right, below: Enthusiasts came from far and wide to photograph and ride on the Chalford auto. A Collett 0-4-2T is waiting to propel its two auto trailers back to Gloucester in this view. The train called at ten stations and halts before arriving in Gloucester Central. It was one of the nine rail motor trains in the timetable from Chalford to Gloucester, while one more started at Brimscombe.

Below: 5041 *Tiverton Castle*, powers its way up the gradient under the skew bridge at milepost 97 beyond Chalford and heads towards Frampton Mansell. With a South Wales based engine in charge, it is possible the train might be one diverted through Gloucester from the Severn Tunnel route due to engineering works. Note the GWR automatic train control ramp under the engine. *George Heiron, The Transport Treasury*

Left, above: A Paddington train at Frampton Mansell is headed by BR 'Britannia' 4-6-2 70015 *Apollo* during the mid-1950s when the loco was shedded at 81A Old Oak Common. Western Region members of the class were regular visitors to Gloucester in their early years; the first was 70019 *Lightning* on 11 August 1951. Following the Milton accident involving 70020 *Mercury*, the WR locos had their smoke deflectors modified; the handrails were removed and replaced with grab holds.
George Heiron, The Transport Treasury

Left, below: This train, approaching Frampton Crossing, appears to be the Fishguard Harbour to Paddington parcels. Assisting the 'Hall' is 2-6-2T 4100, the date is 16 June 1962. Like passenger trains, parcels workings had an assisting engine attached at the front for the ascent of Sapperton. If up freights arrived at Brimscombe double-headed, the leading engine had to detach and assist at the rear to Sapperton Sidings, where it resumed its position at the front.
R S Carpenter collection

Below: An interesting picture showing a permanent way train at Frampton Crossing in Spring 1953. The rails of the up line are being turned so as to counteract wear on the curves. The climb to Sapperton had a lot of reverse curves and heavy trains would have a detrimental effect on the rail profiles. The train, from Swindon, has large Prairie tank 6153 of 81B Slough shed.
P Q Treloar

Above: The banker or assisting engine was not always a tank loco; here it is Mogul 6354 which is pushing a freight headed by 2-8-0 2896 up towards the long tunnel at Sapperton. In the early 1900s, Brimscombe shed sometimes had 'Aberdare' 2-6-0s allocated for banking duties. *R E Toop*

Right, above: Snaking round the curves on the climb up to the tunnels at Sapperton is a ten coach London Paddington train headed by 7903 *Foremarke Hall*, which survives today in preservation. There is no assisting engine, as the load is within the engine's capabilities for keeping to the point-to-point timings for this service. The 'Hall' and 'Modified Hall' classes could take 336 tons between Brimscombe and Kemble, while a 'Castle' could haul 371 tons, about one extra coach. Note the distant signal for down trains, positioned for easy sighting for by drivers coming out of the tunnel.
George Heiron, The Transport Treasury

Right, below: 7004 *Eastnor Castle*, built in June 1946 and allocated new to Gloucester, coasts out of the long tunnel at Sapperton with a Paddington to Cheltenham express on 18 May 1948. Due to the reverse curves on this downhill stretch, passenger trains were restricted to 40mph, while down freights had to come to a dead stand at the nearby 'Stop' board. *H G W Household*

Standish Junction to Tuffley Junction

Left, above: A northbound express from Bristol passes Standish Junction on 2 October 1960 behind BR Standard class 5 73015. The signal box here was extended during the Second World War. Being a Sunday, there is an engineering train occupying the down Midland main line. The crossovers from the Great Western to the Midland lines are prominent. But it was not possible for trains out of Eastgate to access the Swindon route here until a major reorganisation of the junction layout in the autumn of 1964. Once this had been done, Cheltenham to Swindon and London Paddington trains used Eastgate, doing away with the need for the previous reversal – and change of engines – at Gloucester Central station. *H C Casserley*

Left, below: Gloucester 2P 4-4-0 528 has a very light-weight express train at Standish in 1936. It may be the 'special limit' non-stop express which departed Gloucester at 3.35pm for Bath, due there at 4.21pm. This appears from the working time table to have connected with, and possibly been detached from, the 10.20am York to Bristol express due in Gloucester at 3.29pm and departing at 3.40pm. Classmate 527 worked this train in the late 1920s and was 'always resplendent in her maroon livery, must have been the pride of Barnwood's shed.' according to one onlooker.

Below: Heading away from Standish on a northbound freight in LMS days is 4F 4272 of 22B Gloucester, a local engine for many years. It still sports a Fowler chimney; by 1949 it was depicted with the Stanier variety. The train is on the up Midland line to Gloucester, next is the down Midland to Bristol, then the down GWR to Gloucester and up GWR to Swindon. *Real Photographs*

Above: 'Jubilee' 45610 *Gold Coast* speeds along the Midland line approaching Standish Junction with the evening express for Bristol from Newcastle on 26 July 1950. Around this time, 'Jubilees' sometimes worked right through from Bristol to Newcastle on the regular expresses but it proved to be a short-lived experiment, with York being the usual engine changing place. 45610 was shedded at Derby for some years and was a regular at Gloucester, even after it was renamed *Ghana* in 1958. Note the ex-LNER carriages behind the engine. On the right can be seen the start of the two goods loops added here in 1943 to cope with wartime traffic.   *B W L Brooksbank, Initial Photographics*

Right, above: On 29 June 1961 Stanier 8F 2-8-0 48156 of 16B Kirkby-in-Ashfield heads a freight at Haresfield on the down Midland line for Bristol while a GW loco makes for Gloucester on a goods train, probably off the Swindon line.   *S V Blencowe collection*

Right, below: 2-8-0 48010 is passing Haresfield on its way light to Gloucester on 22 August 1957. The station only had platforms on the Midland lines, with four or five trains stopping on weekdays. The 'Trespass' sign is Midland Railway, while the '108' milepost is Great Western Railway, showing the mileage from Paddington. Haresfield was 98 and a half miles from Midland headquarters at Derby.
          H B Priestley collection, Milepost 92$^{1/2}$

Left: The lightly-loaded up afternoon 'Cheltenham Spa Express' to London, seen at Haresfield hauled by semi-streamlined 5005 *Manorbier Castle*, was popularly known as the 'Cheltenham Flyer'. September 1932 saw the 77.3 miles journey from Swindon to Paddington scheduled in 65 minutes, making it the fastest train in the world – but speed between Gloucester and Swindon was rather more mundane, due to the nature of the route. Despite its worldwide fame the 'Cheltenham Flyer' name was never an official one – though it often carried a headboard bearing that name, in black lettering on a white background. *LGRP*

Left, below: Two views just north of Naas Crossing on 13 August 1949 when 96 trains were observed in a seven hour lineside vigil. They depict up trains, both composed of somewhat mixed coaching stock. Double-chimney Ivatt Mogul 43013 is on a special utilising the GW line to bypass Gloucester while 'Crab' 42897 is on the Midland line heading for Eastgate with a Paignton – Newcastle service. The Ivatt was one of half a dozen of the class shedded at Bath Green Park and Bristol Barrow Road at the time, though all had moved on by 1953 – and 43013's somewhat ugly smokestack was replaced by a single chimney, because the locos were poor steamers. The wagons in the background are in Quedgeley sidings; the RAF maintenance establishment they served was opened in 1939 and became a major employer in the area for many years. Trains ran to Quedgeley until after the end of steam and also served the Dow-Mac factory established here in 1963 to manufacture concrete products, including sleepers for BR. *B W L Brooksbank, Initial Photographics*

Above: The Chalford auto heads for Central at Tuffley in August 1959. A train is also signalled on the up line for Eastgate. The Hempsted, or Gloucester New Docks, branch turns off just in front of the signal box. *S Rickard collection, B J Miller*

Below: No wonder the fireman of 0-4-2T 1473 is grinning – his train, the 7.15pm Chalford to Gloucester Central, has just had a fine race all the way from Standish Junction to Tuffley with BR Standard class 5 4-6-0 73096 which is alongside on the 6.30pm passenger from Bristol to Birmingham New Street via Gloucester Eastgate. The Standard had to get up to about 75mph to overtake the auto train according to the photographer. The date is 7 July 1962. *Michael Mensing*

Above: Side window cab Mogul 7338, displaying symptoms of priming, brings the 8.55am Fishguard Harbour to Paddington parcels, with an interesting mix of stock, past Tuffley on 17 June 1960. The small 'Enparts' wagon behind the engine was used for the transport of loco fittings to Swindon Works for attention. The routing of this working is a reminder of pre- Severn Tunnel days when trains from South Wales to London travelled via Gloucester. It was due away from Gloucester Central at 4.48pm, having a scheduled stop there for half an hour; it also stopped at Stroud on the way to Swindon. A couple of passenger and mail trains between London and South Wales were still using the Gloucester route during the night at this date.

M J Jackson

Left, above: A local passenger train, probably a Gloucester to Swindon working, passes Tuffley Junction hauled by ex-works 6820 *Kingstone Grange*. The 2.40pm from Gloucester was often used for locos running in after overhaul at Swindon Works and, indeed, also for brand-new engines constructed there – such as 75000, the first BR Standard Class 4 4-6-0, noted on this train on 7 July 1951.

Left, below: Perhaps BR Standard class 5s do not immediately spring to mind as motive power on London to Gloucester and Cheltenham trains, but Swindon shed had three allocated for a few years from the mid-1950s. This one is 73012 at Tuffley in August 1959 with the service from London on the GW route into Gloucester. The line to Gloucester Eastgate is on the right, while Stroud Road bridge is in the background.

Sid Rickard, Brian Miller collection

There was considerable rivalry at Gloucester between the Great Western and Midland Railways from the earliest days, and this continued despite Nationalisation. The GWR tried to shake off its 'Great Way Round' tag in the early 1900s by building new lines; as a result one new service it offered from July 1908 was from Birmingham to Bristol, in direct competition to the MR who no doubt had become complacent in the running of its train services between these places. But the GWR still had to use the MR's line from Standish Junction to Yate, and, as the MR also controlled the signalling, it is not difficult to guess which service got priority on this section when two trains from the rivals turned up at the same time. At Tuffley, in what looks like a specially posed picture possibly in the summer of 1908, the Midland's 4-4-0 751 sweeps out of Gloucester while the GWR's 4-4-0 3406 *Melbourne* runs alongside, both said to be on Birmingham to Bristol expresses. But the GWR's did not call at Gloucester, instead it ran via Gloucester South.   *V R Webster collection, Kidderminster Railway Museum*

The five mile section between Tuffley and Standish often saw the spectacle of trains racing each other when the GWR train was heading for the Stroud Valley line and the Midland for the Bristol line. One favourite race was that of a Collett 0-4-2T on the one-coach Chalford auto dashing along at 70mph with the full-throated roar of a 3-cylinder Stanier 'Jubilee' alongside on a cross-country express. Even seasoned observers like E L Ahrons, the distinguished locomotive historian and former pupil of Mr W. Dean at Swindon Locomotive Works, revelled in the thrill of the chase:

'The races were very exciting at times, and generally speaking honours were fairly evenly divided. The Great Western Railway men used to say that the Midland engines had an advantage, for the latter ran on a transverse sleeper road, whereas the Great Western Railway piece in question was at that time (the nineteenth century) laid entirely on longitudinal baulk road, which was 'dead' and not elastic to run over. The Gloucester drivers of the 7ft (2-2-2) singles *Beaconsfield* and *Salisbury* were frequently upset because two Midland 0-4-4 tank engines, 1280 and 1281 with 5ft 6 inches wheels, used to show them a clean pair of heels. These Midland engines worked a light local train from Gloucester to Lydney via the Severn Bridge, and started out from Gloucester about the same time as the New Milford up boat train left for London. But *Beaconsfield* and *Salisbury* occasionally took their revenge by beating a Bristol train on the down journey. Personally, I had a good many 'scraps' over this section. But I must confess to catching a very bad Tartar one night on loco 2201 (a 2-4-0) with the up South Wales – London mail, when, although we ran from Gloucester to Stroud, 12 miles, in 14 minutes, we were badly beaten by Midland engine 816 on a Bristol express. But this particular Midland engine was one of a celebrated class (of 4-4-0s), which in their day were second to none in the whole country, and luckily for our reputation on the Great Western Railway there were none of them except 816 stationed by the Midland in the West – and this one was only there for a year or two.'

Looking out of the roundhouse at Barnwood depot into the yard, with a group of enthusiasts taking it all in on an official visit. The date is 12 August 1960, the loco in the centre is 4F 44167 and Engine Shed Junction signal box is in the background.

B J Miller collection

Acknowledgements

Quite a number of people have helped to expand my own knowledge of the Gloucester area railway system and its history and operation.My thanks for their contributions to Jim Irwin, Mike Randall, Dave Smith and Derek Smith who all worked on the footplate at Gloucester, Dick Etherton, Roy Smith, Roger Wales and Peter Witts. Photographs have come from various sources and I am grateful to all who supplied them, including the late Brian Miller, Dick Courtney, Bob Pixton, Ben Ashworth, Audie Baker of Kidderminster Railway Museum, Tony Bowles of the Restoration & Archiving Trust – Toddington, Alan Jarvis particularly for the very fine front cover picture, and Alan Lewis Chambers who has an excellent website displaying some of his photos, including two used in this book. For local information on locomotive and train workings, reports in the RTCS 'Railway Observer' and the newsletters of the Gloucestershire Raiway Society over a number of years have been very helpful, as have many official railway publications such as the Gloucester Traffic District Sectional Appendix and Working Time Tables etc.

Bibliography

The Birmingham and Gloucester Railway
  P J Long and Rev W V Awdrey

Bristol and Gloucester Railway Colin Maggs

A Regional History of the Railways of Great Britain Vol. 13 Thames and Severn Rex Christiansen

The Midland Railway – A Chronology John Gough

Midland Railway System Maps – Birmingham to Bristol and Branches

Track Layout Diagrams of the GWR and BR WR
  R A Cooke

Pre-Grouping Railway Junction Diagrams 1914

British Railway Locomotives 1948 Chris Banks

Passengers No More Gerald Daniels and Les Dench

Locomotive and Train Working in the Latter Part of the Nineteenth Century E L Ahrons

Midland Record Preview Issue – Coaley Junction for Dursley Roger Carpenter